MODELING STRUCTURES

Jeff Wilson

Kalmbach Books
21027 Crossroads Circle
Waukesha, Wisconsin 53186
www.Kalmbach.com/Books

© 2016 Kalmbach Books
All rights reserved. This book may not be reproduced in part or in whole by any means whether electronic or otherwise without written permission of the publisher except for brief excerpts for review.

Published in 2016
20 19 18 17 16   1 2 3 4 5

Manufactured in China

ISBN: 978-1-62700-223-3
EISBN: 978-1-62700-225-7

Editor: Randy Rehberg
Book Design: Tom Ford

Unless noted, photographs were taken by the author.

Library of Congress Control Number: 2015941326

Contents

Introduction 4

Chapter 1
Tools and adhesives 5

Chapter 2
Structure kits 13

Chapter 3
Modular and kitbashed structures 26

Chapter 4
Scratchbuilding 35

Chapter 5
Interior detailing and lighting 49

Chapter 6
Painting and weathering 59

Chapter 7
Signs 72

Chapter 8
Structures and flats from photos 82

Chapter 9
Finishing scenes 90

List of manufacturers 94

About the author 95

Acknowledgments 95

By giving structures unique names and detailing, you can set them apart from otherwise identical models. This HO building is marketed as a hobby shop by Walthers, but I turned it into a TV and appliance store by adding some interior details, a new exterior wall sign, and a hanging sign made from a photograph. The window signs—made from old advertising materials—make it apparent that it's the early 1960s.

Introduction

As stationary models, structures are, in effect, part of a layout's scenery. Structures help set the tone and mood of a layout, as they establish the era, region, and often the exact town or locale of a layout or scene.

More and more structures are becoming available in built-up form, but there's still a tremendous variety of structures still available in kit form. These range from basic (four walls and a roof) plastic kits to complex plastic, resin, or wood models with hundreds of pieces. And with the Internet, it's easier than ever to track down out-of-production kits, materials, and details through eBay and other online sources.

If you're just getting into the hobby, building a simple plastic structure kit is a great way to get started in model building. The beauty of building a structure kit is that, unlike a freight car or locomotive, it doesn't need to stay on the track: you have more of a margin for error. Building a basic structure gives you experience in working with basic tools, adhesives, paints, and other materials—and helps build confidence for your next model.

The beauty of modeling structures is that there are so many ways of customizing them, making them unique to your layout (and different from the thousands of otherwise-identical models on other layouts across the country). The way you paint and weather them; add interior details and lighting; and personalize them with signs—all add to realism and make structures distinctive.

As with many other facets of the hobby, you can take structure modeling and detailing to any level you desire. In general, the larger your layout, the more you have to concentrate on the overall effect as opposed to giving every model a high level of detail. However, if you have a smaller layout with fewer structures, you can get more adventurous with weathering, interiors, lighting, and other details.

Although this book does have a few how-to projects in it, it is designed as an idea book—the techniques, ideas, and concepts are meant to apply to any project you're working on. Likewise, although most of the models in this book are HO scale, the fundamentals carry across all scales.

1

CHAPTER ONE

Tools and adhesives

Having the proper tools is essential in getting good results when building structures (or any other models, for that matter), **1**. There's a tremendous variety of tools available, ranging from basic to complex. We'll start with a look at a list of basic modeling tools for beginners and then check out some nice specialty tools that are handy to have. We'll also look at the strengths and proper uses for various glues and adhesives.

Using the correct tools makes most hobby tasks much easier, resulting in better models. Here, a Coffman corner clamp holds two HO plastic structure walls together to ensure proper alignment while applying glue.

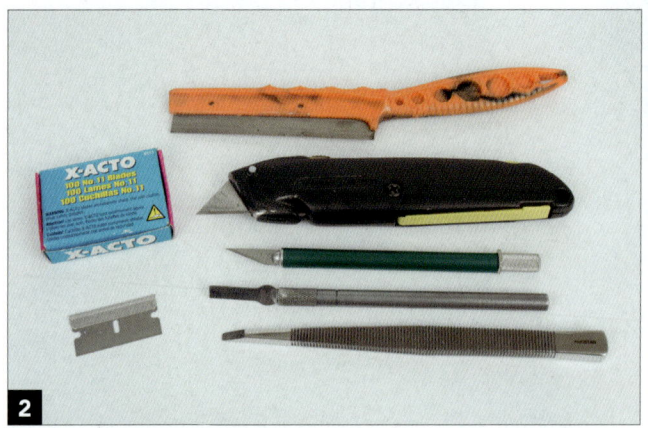

Vital cutting tools include (from top) a razor saw, utility knife, and hobby knives with no. 11 and no. 17 blades. The modeler's chisel (at bottom) from Micro-Mark enables precision removal of plastic details. Safety razor blades (left) are also handy.

When the tip breaks off a hobby knife blade, discard it safely and install a new blade.

Hobby knives

The first item on the modeling tool list is a good hobby knife, **2**. X-Acto has almost become synonymous with hobby knife, but Excel and others offer them as well. The most common blade is the no. 11, a pointed-end blade with a sharp angle at the tip. The no. 11 works well for most general cutting, slicing, and scraping jobs. Its biggest weakness is the fine-point tip—it tends to break off rather easily, **3**.

The key to achieving good results with a hobby knife is to maintain a sharp blade. If the blade becomes dull or the tip breaks, discard it and install a new one. Dull or broken blades won't cut cleanly, leaving jagged edges on cut lines, and they can easily slip and damage models. Some modelers sharpen their old blades, and although this is certainly possible, I'd rather spend my time modeling instead of sharpening old blades.

These blades are cheap if you buy them in bulk—boxes of 100 are economical, and by buying them this way, you won't worry if you have to replace them frequently.

Another commonly used blade is the no. 17, which has a squared-off chisel shape. This blade works well for removing parts from sprues, chopping wood and plastic strips, and shaving and removing details from flat surfaces. Invest in two handles (one for each blade) so you don't waste time changing blades as you need them. Don't simply throw old blades into the garbage: buy a sharps container and dispose of them safely.

Hobby knives are rather light for some cutting jobs. Keep a general-service utility knife handy for cutting heavy sheet styrene and wood (.060" or thicker), kit walls, mat board and other heavy cardboard, and foam core. These blades are thicker and heavier than hobby knife blades, and their shallower angle makes them less prone to broken tips. As with hobby knives, change the blades frequently.

Some modelers prefer surgical scalpels for modeling work. Scalpel blades are extremely sharp, and they are thinner, harder, and will stay sharp longer than hobby blades. I personally don't like the feel of them, but they are worth consideration.

Single-edge razor blades are also useful, as they are extremely sharp and thinner than hobby blades. Some tools (such as the NorthWest Short Line Chopper) also employ them.

Scale rules

A scale rule is a vital piece of equipment, making it unnecessary to remember formulae to convert prototype measurements to scale inches, **4**. General, Mascot, X-Acto, and others make 6"- and 12"-long steel rules with markings for multiple scales. These are good for transferring dimensions from drawings to the work in progress. Steel rules make good straightedge guides for cutting and marking.

Safety

Most people know they should wear eye protection when using power tools such as a motor tool, power saw, or drill press.

It's also a good idea to put on safety glasses when using manual tools. Tips of knife blades and drill bits can break and go flying, and bits of metal and plastic from filing can become airborne.

Heed instructions on glues, adhesives, and paint regarding solvent vapors. Many are harmful to breathe, so work in a well-ventilated area and/or wear a cartridge-style respirator when using them (also when soldering). These solvents are also flammable, so be sure to use them away from sources of ignition (such as water heaters and furnaces).

Always use care when working with hobby knives and other sharp tools. Keep yourself (and your free hand and fingers) away from the blade path in case it slips.

Finally, always keep tools and solvents away from children and pets. If you have toddlers or small children, keep your workshop door closed and locked or keep items in locked cabinets.

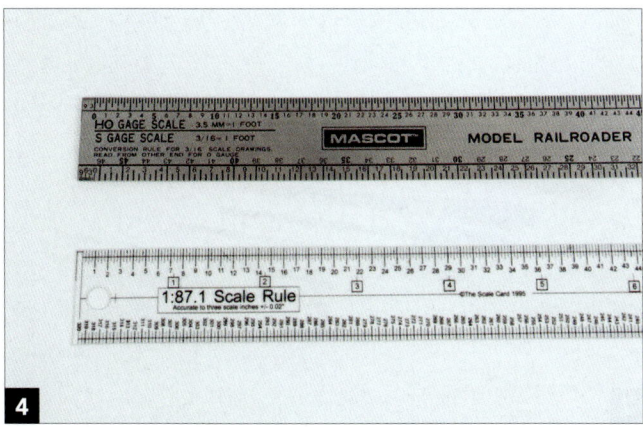

4 Steel and clear plastic scale rules are available from several manufacturers. Most have markings for multiple scales.

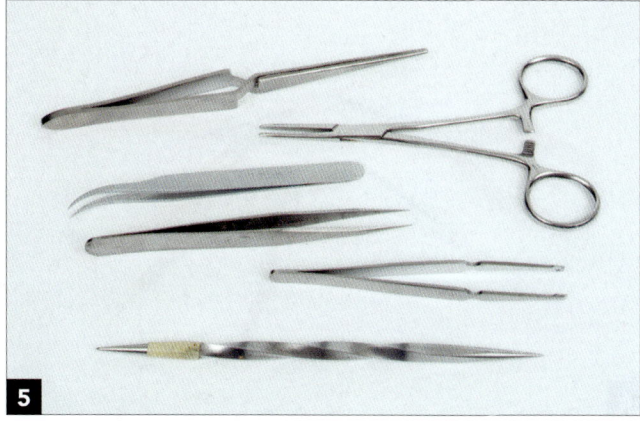

5 Types of tweezers include (from top) cross-locking, hemostat, curved-tip, standard pointed, and notched-tip. A double-ended scriber, shown at the bottom, is a useful tool for removing material.

Microscale and others make clear plastic scale rules in various sizes. I find these especially handy for checking dimensions on drawings and complex shapes, as you can lay them directly across drawings and actual models to get accurate measurements.

Tweezers, pliers, and cutters

Even when working in large scales, you'll quickly discover that your fingers are too big for holding and positioning many model parts. Tweezers are handy for moving, holding, and applying details, as well as holding parts in position for painting and gluing, **5**.

By far, the handiest are standard 3"- or 4"-long tweezers with straight fine points. Other versions you may find useful are curved-tip tweezers and angled-tip tweezers, which are good for getting into odd-shaped places. Tweezers with notches in the tip can be used for grabbing round parts that tend to slip out of standard tweezers.

Along with pointed tips, you'll find tweezers with squared, rounded, and angled tips, as well as cross-locking tweezers, which are normally closed and require pressure to open. Another version of these, called soldering tweezers, is similar but has wood or other material on the grips to dissipate heat.

The hemostat is a relative of a tweezers. Hemostats have fine tips and can be locked in the closed position. A series of notches in the handle allows you to vary the pressure of the locked position.

Pliers are heavier and stronger than tweezers, and are useful for holding parts, bending wire (as well as strip and sheet metal), and making adjustments on other tools, **6**. Needle-nose pliers have a fine tip, and versions are available in several sizes, with curved and bent tips, and with or without serrations on the jaws. You'll also find many uses for standard square-jaw pliers.

Side cutters in various sizes can be used for removing parts from sprues, for cutting rail, and for cutting wire and strip metal. Side cutters are available in two styles: those with blades that butt at the cutting point, and those with blades that cut in a shearing motion. Most standard wire cutters use butting blades, but those marketed as sprue cutters or rail cutters (such as the Xuron tool shown in photo **6**) use shearing action, which results in a clean cut on the outward edge.

Don't cut music wire or other steel strip material with standard sprue cutters or wire cutters, as the material will ding and damage the blades. Special cutters are available for steel wire.

Tweezer-style sprue cutters are great for most lightweight plastic sprues, and will leave a very clean cut with little cleanup needed. They are available from Micro-Mark and others in standard versions or those having extended points for getting into tight areas.

Files and sanders

Building structures—whether kits or scratchbuilt—requires a lot of cutting, filing, and shaping of walls, roofs, and strip and sheet material. Files of various sizes and with different cutting patterns are valuable tools, **7**. I keep a full-size (10") fine mill file and a crosscut bastard file at hand. The coarser bastard file is great for removing material relatively quickly, while the fine mill file cleans up edges and removes any marks made from coarser files.

Smaller files, including 8", 6", and 4", as well as needle files and jeweler's files, are great for getting into tight spaces and small openings. They are made in a variety of shapes, including flat, round, oval, square, and triangular, and have fine to coarse cutting surfaces.

Sanding sticks are invaluable in structure building, **8**. The basic disposable, abrasive fingernail file is inexpensive (or free, as they are often used as giveaway items) and good for smoothing and shaping edges and parts. You can also buy finer nail-shaping pads, some of which have multiple grits on the same stick. Squadron, X-Acto, and others make rigid and flexible sanding sticks ranging from 800-grit to 1,500-grit and even 12,000-grit.

You'll also find yourself using sandpaper on a regular basis. Sandpaper is graded in coarseness by grit (the number of grit particles per

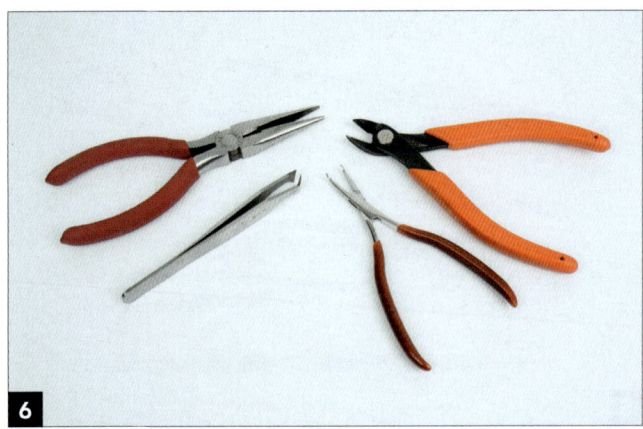

6 Pliers and cutters can be used for a variety of modeling tasks. From left are needle-nose pliers, a tweezer-style sprue cutter, fine-tip needle-nose pliers, and shear-action side cutters (Xuron).

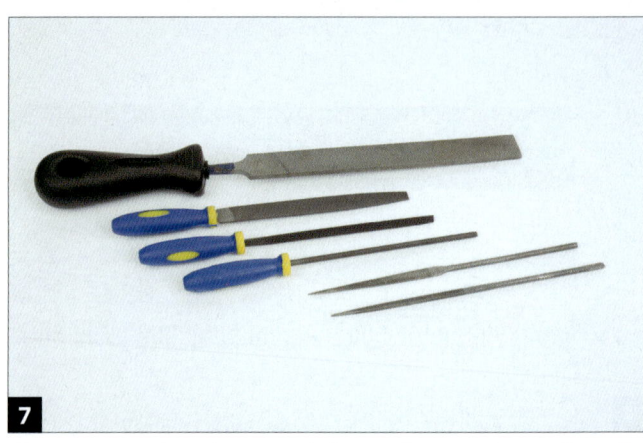

7 Files come in several sizes and shapes (from top): a 6" flat mill, 4" flat, triangular, round, and flat-angled and oval needle files.

inch). Thus, the lower the number, the coarser the paper (and the larger the grit size). For model railroading purposes, 120-grit is coarse, 220 or 240 is medium, and 400 is fine; 600- through 1,000-grit and finer paper and sticks can be used for polishing.

In general, when sanding surfaces, start with coarse grit, then move to gradually finer grits until the edge or surface is as smooth as needed. Modelers also often use sandpaper to roughen glossy surfaces. For example, when using styrene sheet to represent an asphalt or concrete roadway or tarred roof, sanding it in a circular pattern with 120- or 220-grit paper will give it a more realistic texture.

You can use pieces of sandpaper by themselves, but I like using standard carpenter's sanding blocks. These rubber pads hold a piece of sandpaper evenly on surfaces, and save your hands from the friction of the paper and surface.

Pin vise and drill bits

You'll often find the need to drill holes of various sizes for mounting and fitting parts and detail items. Small drill bits are sized by number: the larger the number, the smaller the bit, **9**. A typical set of modeler's drill bits includes sizes 61 (.039") through 80 (.0135").

Carbon steel bits are common in low-priced sets, and they work fine for wood, resin, and plastic but will dull quickly in brass and other metal. High-speed steel (HSS) bits are pricier, but they're more durable and will stay sharper longer, even while cutting metal. Buying an initial set of carbon bits is an economical approach. As they break or become dull (or if you have a specific need for cutting metal), you can replace them as needed with individual HSS bits.

To drill smaller holes, use a small manual tool called a pin vise. Available in several styles, you'll be able to find one that fits comfortably in your hand. To use it, place the bit in the chuck and tighten the collar. Leave only as much of the bit exposed as needed for the hole you're drilling.

Hold the pin vise perpendicular to the surface with your index finger on the end. Rotate the bit with your thumb and middle finger, applying light pressure with your index finger. Work slowly—don't force pressure, and make sure the pin vise and bit don't bend while drilling, as these small bits break very easily. Marking a starting point with an awl or a scriber aids in accuracy. Pause frequently to remove cut material.

A pin vise can be used with larger bits as well (up to ⅛" with many tools).

Miscellaneous tools

I keep my workbench protected with a self-healing cutting mat. These are available in a variety of sizes (one of my green ones is visible in many photos throughout the book). A self-healing mat protects hobby knives, letting the tips penetrate without damage, and they make it easy to hold materials in place while cutting.

I like to keep one mat in pristine condition for precise work, such as trimming decals and paper, and keep another one for general workbench use. Over time, they get dinged up and tend to get covered in glue and paint spatters. When that happens, discard the one on your workbench and rotate a new one into service.

A razor saw has a much thinner blade with finer teeth than a standard crosscut saw or hacksaw, **2**. Razor saws work well for cutting strip material, including wide, heavy plastic, wood, and brass tubing. Using one with a small miter box produces precise, square cuts. You can also use a steel straightedge to guide one across wider surfaces.

Square cuts are essential when trimming and sizing walls, roofs, and other structure components. Among my most-used tools is a common carpenter's combination square, **10**. With it, and a hobby or utility knife, you can easily and precisely cut styrene sheet, mat board, and other materials. A small steel machinist's square is also handy for the same reasons, as is a speed square that also provides markings for various other angles. I also like to use a clear plastic drafting square as a straightedge for cutting. The see-through property makes it easy to align cuts precisely, especially for decals or paper signs.

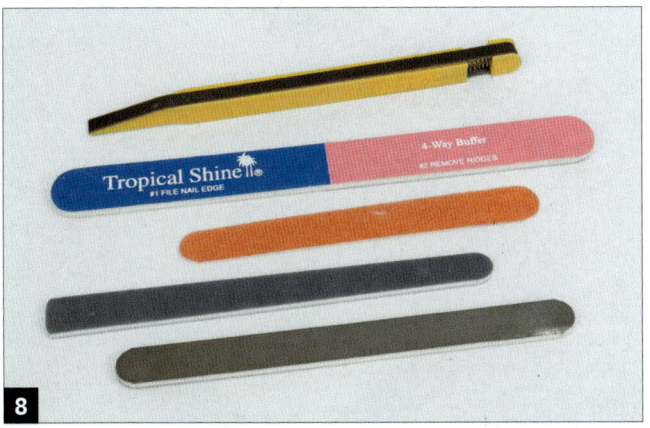

8 Sanding sticks include (from top) an X-Acto version with replaceable sanding belts, a four-grit flexible nail file, an inexpensive rigid nail file, and flexible sanding sticks from Squadron that come in various grits.

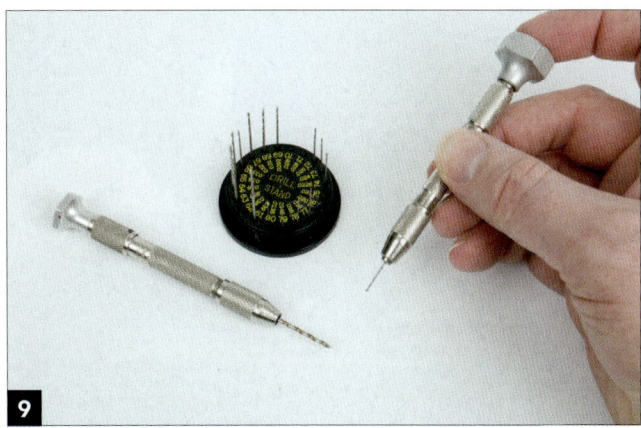

9 Pin vises—miniature manual drills with small bits—make it easy to drill small holes in plastic and other materials. Start with a set of nos. 61–80 bits.

Specialty tools

A number of tools aren't truly necessary if you're only interested in building basic structure kits. However, the more structures you build—and the more additional detailing, kitbashing, and scratchbuilding you do—the more you will find yourself needing or wanting additional specialty tools that help with specific jobs. Some are expensive, others aren't, but how many you opt for is determined by your budget and available workshop space.

High on this list for me are a pair of tools from NorthWest Short Line: the Chopper and the True Sander. The Chopper is basically a miniature miter saw, with a razor blade on a handle in place of a rotating saw blade, **11**.

The Chopper has several angle attachments that can be clamped to the cutting fence, and stop blocks can be used to allow cutting multiple identical parts. This tool makes short work of any styrene or wood strip material (or thin sheet material) with minimal cleanup needed on the cut edges. I consider it a necessity when scratchbuilding.

The True Sander has an aluminum sanding block that slides perpendicular to a guide fence, which allows precise sanding of almost any strip or sheet material (including walls and roofs), **12**. An adjustable guide in a slot allows you to sand material at any angle. Any grade of sandpaper can be used on the multifaced block. I keep coarse sandpaper on one side and fine sandpaper on the other.

Clamps are useful when gluing building parts together, **13**. Available in several sizes, Coffman Engineering's Corner Clamps are great for joining walls together—which can be one of the trickier challenges of building structures, **1**. They hold two pieces at a 90-degree angle, and the back of the clamp is open, which allows you to apply glue.

Another specialty clamp is the adjustable corner clamp (Pony is one brand). These can be adjusted to any angle. They're designed for building picture frames, but are great for holding roof sections and wall joints at other than 90-degree junctions.

Small sliding bar clamps (such as Quick-Grips) and spring clamps of various sizes are handy for holding things together, from two mating surfaces for gluing up to entire structure assemblies.

The Plastic Modeler's Chisel from Micro-Mark is a great tool for cleanly removing details from any plastic surface, **2**. Its design results in a much cleaner cut (with little chance of gouging) compared to a flat modeler's knife. They're made with two blade widths: 4mm (no. 80893) and 2mm (no. 82709).

Many modelers invest in a handheld motor tool, **14**. Dremel is the most popular brand, and the company offers many models. Get one with a speed control built in, as the top speed on most motor tools is much too fast for drilling holes and other basic jobs.

Think of motor tools more like miniature routers than drills: their biggest strength is grinding and cutting with various-shaped routing bits, grinding bits, and cutoff wheels. They can also be used with drill bits at low speeds. (Always wear eye protection when using a motor tool).

You may not need a drill press very often, but they're wonderful if you need a hole drilled precisely (or if you need a lot of holes drilled at one time). I love my miniature Micro-Lux press, available (along with many others) from Micro-Mark.

Measuring the thickness of walls, roofs, and sheet or strip material is easy with a dial caliper, **15**. The design of a caliper allows measuring either outside (measuring the thickness of sheet and strip material or wire) or inside (the width of a hole or window opening). Most are marked in thousandths of an inch. (General once offered versions marked in HO and O scale, but they haven't been available for several years.)

Keep your eyes open when shopping in the tool section in your favorite hardware store, or go online to the Micro-Mark catalog (micromark.com) and poke around—you never know when you might come across another tool that you may deem essential!

Glues

Bonding things together is an important part of structure assembly. Choosing the right adhesive—and using it properly and carefully—results

Squares aid in cutting and assembly. From left are a 7" speed square, small machinist's square, combination square, and clear 30/60/90 drafting square.

NorthWest Short Line's Chopper serves as a miniature miter saw, with a razor blade in place of a saw blade. Shown here is the Chopper II version, which features a self-healing cutting mat (the original has a hardboard surface).

in a solid joint and sturdy model; choosing the wrong adhesive can lead to sloppy joints and models that fall apart, and careless use of glues can mar or stain a model.

There are many types of adhesives on the market today, and each works well with different materials. The key is matching the glue to the material, and choosing the proper one when bonding dissimilar items.

Plastic cement

Plastic is the most common material in kits, raw materials, and detail items, so let's start with a look at plastic cement. Plastic cement comes in two basic forms: liquid and gel, **16**. Liquid is thinner than water, and it comes in small bottles, often with an applicator brush on the inner cap. Gel is thicker, and it is applied through a tube applicator built into the bottle. (It may be called *liquid*, as the Testor's Liquid Cement for Plastic Models shown in the photo.)

Both types work the same way. They are not adhesives, so the glue itself doesn't hold parts together. Instead, plastic cement melts the mating plastic surfaces and causes the plastic to melt together. The result is an extremely strong bond. Because plastic cements dissolve the plastic surface (as well as paint), it's important to never get stray glue on a model's surface.

To work properly, the mating pieces should be bare (unpainted). Carefully scrape off any paint from the mating surfaces, or better yet, mask areas that you know will be glued prior to painting.

Liquid-type cement is meant to be applied to joints that can be held together. Apply cement carefully with a brush, and capillary action will draw the liquid into the joint. Continue holding the parts for several seconds until the cement begins to set. Clamps can be used to hold joints securely.

Use gel-type cement by applying it to one surface or edge. Press the other part in place and hold it for a few seconds. Don't apply so much that it oozes out of the joint when the parts are joined.

Liquid cement is especially useful for hidden joints, where touching the surface with a brush won't disturb visible areas (such as the inside of a corner between two walls). Gel is good any time you need to precisely place a part on a visible surface.

Plastic cement will last indefinitely if you keep the lid closed and the bottle capped.

Super glue and epoxy

Super glue, more technically called cyanoacrylate adhesive or CA, is a good multipurpose glue for joining metal, resin, and plastic to other materials, **17**. Super glue is available in several viscosities, from super thin and thin (thinner than water) to medium, thick, and gap-filling. It bonds quickly: instantly for thin CA, a few seconds for medium, and 15 to 20 seconds for thick and gap-filling.

I find medium to be the best general-purpose CA. It can be applied directly with the bottle's applicator, but you'll have more control if you put a few drops on a scrap piece of plastic or card and apply it with a toothpick or pin.

I usually reach for CA whenever plastic cement won't work: when attaching dissimilar materials (such as brass to plastic, plastic to wood, or wood to brass), or when gluing resin parts. It also works well on wood, and provides a quicker bond than wood glue. You shouldn't use general-purpose CA on foam, as it will dissolve it (although foam-safe CAs are now available). Some CAs are designed for plastic-to-plastic joints, which is handy for attaching details to larger models.

Super glue accelerator—generally available in small spray bottles—can be used to instantly cure CA. Be sure nothing on the surface will be affected by the accelerator (it can dissolve some paints and stain some materials). You can also apply a drop or two to a joint with a pipette. Do not apply more super glue once you've applied accelerator; simply touching the bottle tip to the accelerator can cause a good share of the bottle to cure instantly.

Super glue also works well for filling gaps. I use it often instead of conventional plastic putty. Apply thick or gap-filling CA to an opening or gap—work in layers if the space is large (more than 1⁄16" or so)—and

12 The True Sander uses an aluminum block with sandpaper applied to it, together with a fence, to get precise, square edges on sheet and strip material.

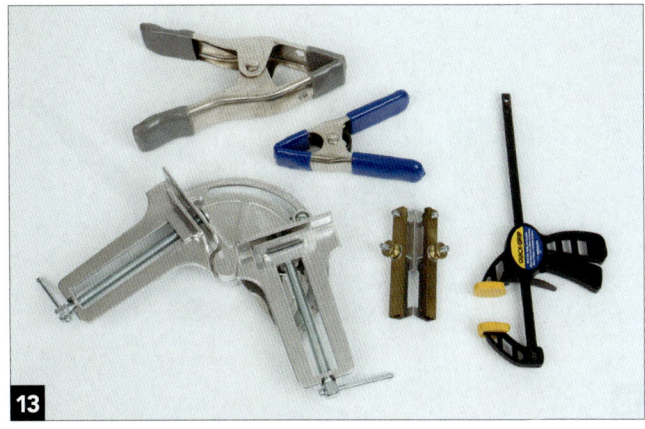

13 Helpful clamps include (clockwise from top) various sizes of spring clamps, small quick-action bar clamps (this is a Quick-Grip), Coffman's Corner Clamp, and an adjustable-angle corner clamp.

14 Motor tools are great for drilling, grinding, and sanding. Their cutoff disks can make short work of cutting brass and other metals.

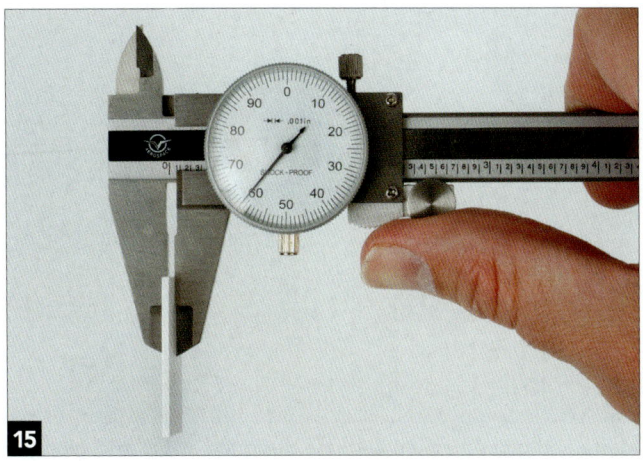

15 A dial caliper is handy for taking precise measurements of sheet and dimensional material, as well as for measuring openings.

apply accelerator. Wipe off any excess accelerator and then use shaping tools, such as an emery board, file, sanding block, or knife to carve the CA to match the surface.

Don't use CA to glue clear styrene, and don't use it in an enclosed small space near clear styrene windows, as CA's vapors can frost and fog clear styrene.

Air (especially if the humidity is high) is the enemy of CA. Keep bottles capped when not in use. Even when doing that, you can plan on about three months of use from a bottle after it's opened, so buy only as much as you think you'll use in that time. If the CA becomes thicker or stringy, or if it's taking noticeably longer to cure, discard the bottle and open a new one.

Epoxy is a clear two-part compound that dries clear and glossy. Mixing the epoxy and the hardener activates it. The cure time varies by type, but a 5-minute cure is common. Epoxy is good for nonporous materials such as metal and resin, and it is generally stronger than CA. The tradeoff is that it takes more time (mixing and waiting for cure) than CA. Parts need to be clamped or held in place, as epoxy doesn't bond quickly.

Apply equal parts hardener and epoxy to a piece of plain card or plastic. Use a large wood toothpick or stir stick to thoroughly mix the two for at least a minute—if they aren't thoroughly mixed, the epoxy may not completely cure, which can create a big mess. Epoxy becomes cloudy with tiny air bubbles as it's mixed, but it becomes clear as it dries.

Epoxy has a long shelf life. Just remember that once it's mixed, there's no way to extend the cure time. Apply it carefully with a toothpick, making sure to get it exactly where you want it, as stray epoxy can easily mar a surface.

White and wood glues

White glue is water-based. It's generally a good choice for bonding porous materials such as wood, paper, cardstock, and mat board, **18**. It works by penetrating the pores in the material to create a bond. It will not work on plastic, metal, resin, and other nonporous materials.

Wood glue (also known as yellow glue, carpenter's glue, and aliphatic resin glue) has greater strength than white glue and is resistant to water after curing. It's a good choice for wood-to-wood joints.

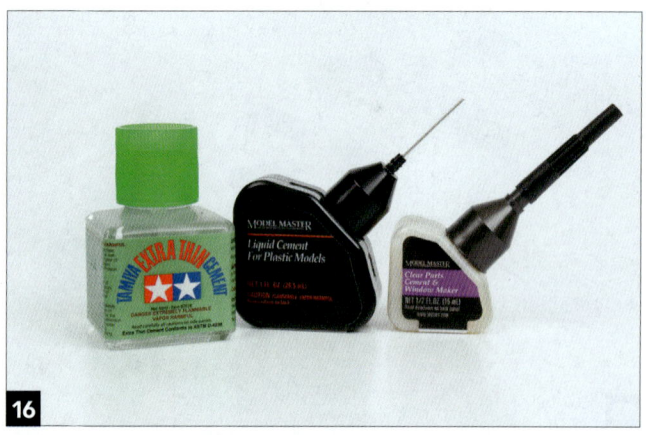

16 Plastic cements include thin liquids, such as Tamiya Extra Thin Cement (left), and gel-type glues such as Model Master Liquid Cement for Plastic Models. Model Master Clear Parts Cement is designed for gluing clear styrene.

17 Super glue (cyanoacrylate adhesive, or CA) is available in viscosities from thin to thick. It cures instantly when accelerator is added (left). Epoxy (right) comes in two parts that must be thoroughly mixed.

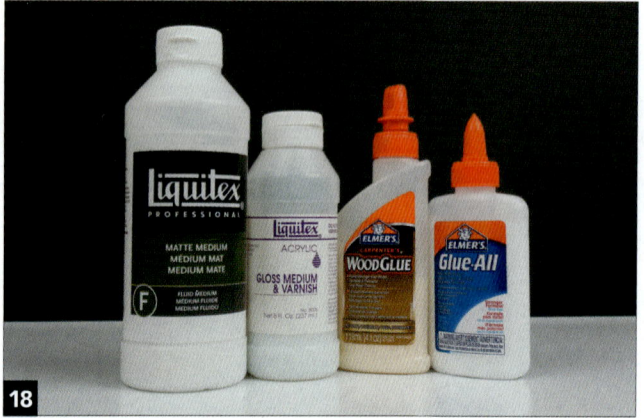

18 Matte and gloss medium (left) are designed as flat and glossy finishes for surfaces, but they can also be used to glue porous materials. Aliphatic resin (wood) glue bonds wood tightly, and white glue (right) can be used with most porous materials.

19 Other adhesives (from left) include rubber cement, general-purpose glues such as Gorilla Glue and E6000, Woodland Scenics Accent Glue, and vinyl and resin cement.

With either type of glue, the joint must be tight—neither wood glue nor white glue is good at filling gaps. Clamp the work together if possible, as it takes several minutes for both types of glue to set and several hours to cure.

Matte medium and gloss medium are designed as finish coatings for artists. Both are water-based and can be used for gluing porous materials if you need glue that has either a flat or glossy sheen.

If you're planning to stain wood, do so before applying any of these glues, as the glue will seal the pores in wood and prevent the stain from penetrating.

Other adhesives

Rubber cement is good for gluing sheets of material to each other, such as paper or cardboard, **19**. To use rubber cement, brush a coat on both surfaces to be joined. Wait several minutes, until the cement on both surfaces is dry to the touch, and then carefully position the material and press into place, using a roller if possible to secure the bond.

Multiuse general-purpose adhesives can bond dissimilar materials. Polyurethane glue (Gorilla Glue) and E6000 can both be used on a variety of materials including wood, metal, ceramic, glass, and many plastics (but not foam for E6000). They work well with a stronger bond than CA, but they don't bond quickly—it takes 4 or 5 minutes for these glues to set and up to 24 hours to cure. Where great strength isn't needed, CA is usually a quicker alternative.

Accent Glue from Woodland Scenics is great when you need a temporary or removable, low-strength bond. It looks like white glue. Dab a bit on a part and let it dry for a couple of minutes. It will stay tacky, letting you position the part in place but allowing you to easily remove it. It's great for setting figures and other details in scenes where you want them to stay put but don't want them in place permanently.

Spray adhesives (3M Super 77 is one type) work well for joining large flat surfaces, such as securing a photo print of a building to a backdrop. They can be messy (the spray can get anywhere, so spray over newspapers or outside), and pieces can be hard to handle. You need to get the alignment perfect on the first try because, once the glue grabs, you won't be able to move the material.

1

CHAPTER TWO

Structure kits

Kits are available in all scales to represent almost any type of structure in real life, from railroad-specific buildings like depots and roundhouses to storefront buildings, factories, and houses, **1**. Model kits range from extremely simple—four walls and a roof—to complex buildings with hundreds of components and detail parts.

Kits can be found in a variety of railroad and non-railroad-related buildings, and many are based on actual structures. This HO model is built from a laser-cut wood kit by GC Laser. It's based on the Chicago Great Western depot that once served Peru, Ill.

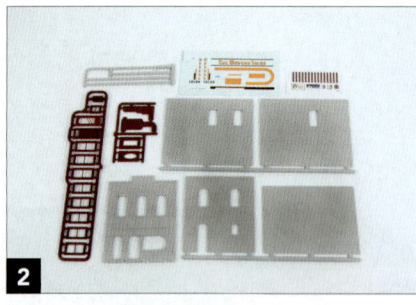

2 Take a quick inventory of all kit parts and become familiar with them. This HO storefront building from City Classics is a basic kit and contains walls, a roof, and window and door castings, as well as signs and graphics.

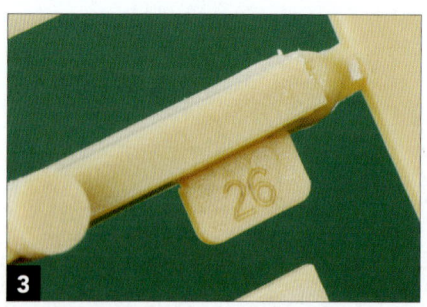

3 Sprues often include identification numbers next to their respective parts. Leave the parts on the sprues until you need them.

4 A hobby knife with a straight blade (no. 17) works well for removing parts from sprues (and mold gates from parts). Working on a self-healing cutting mat helps preserve blades.

5 Tweezer-style cutters, like these from Micro-Mark, cut parts from sprues very cleanly. They work best on small, thin sprues.

6 Larger sprue cutters, like these from Xuron, look like wire cutters, but they cut with a shearing action. They can be used on large parts and thick sprues.

7 Carefully shave any sprue remnants from parts with a sharp hobby knife. Go slowly and use several passes to avoid gouging parts.

8 You can use a sanding stick or file to clean up sprue marks or touch up areas where you use a knife.

Kits are made from a variety of materials, but the bulk of them are wood or injection-molded plastic. Resin, metal, and plaster are also used as primary building materials. Mass-produced plastic kits have been produced since the 1950s, and indeed, some individual kits have been around since that time—often appearing under the labels of many manufacturers. Other kits have been produced in limited runs, a practice especially true for wood and resin buildings.

The best way to get started with building structures is with a simple plastic kit. Whether an injection-molded kit has a dozen pieces or 300, the steps are the same. Once you get the hang of basic modeling techniques, you can move to a more complex

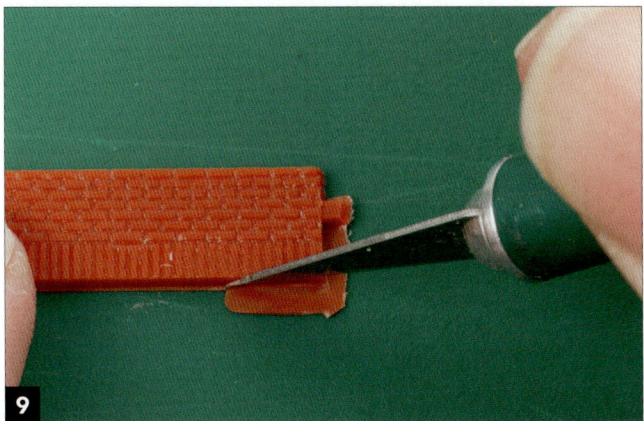

Flash is stray plastic that oozes out along the mold seams. Trim it away with a knife and then file or smooth the area if necessary.

Use a brush (in this case, the brush inside the bottle cap) to apply liquid plastic cement to the joint between a window frame and the wall. Capillary action draws the liquid into the joint. Do this at the rear (nonvisible area) of a joint.

Gel-type cement is good for adding details, such as this brick panel on a wall face. Use the bottle's applicator to apply the cement along the part.

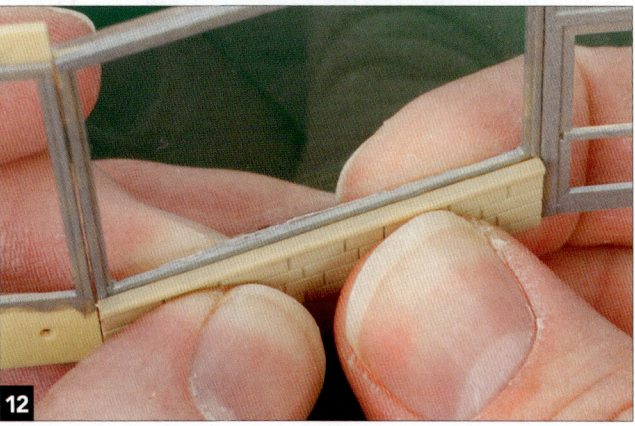

Making sure the alignment is correct, press the part in place until the joint holds.

plastic kit and then to a laser-cut wood kit, a resin kit, or a modified or scratchbuilt structure.

Basic steps

When starting a kit, it's tempting to just dive in and start putting the pieces together. However, regardless of the material, scale, and prototype, there are a few basic steps you should do before getting out the knife and glue. The first is removing all the parts from the package and taking a quick inventory, **2**. Make sure all of the parts are there—parts sometimes fall off sprues, or a kit might be missing individual components. Also familiarize yourself with the parts—two or more parts might appear identical when in fact they are not.

Instructions can range from a simple exploded-isometric diagram to multiple pages of detailed step-by-step assembly. If you're reasonably new to the hobby, first read through all the instructions. And even if you're an experienced modeler, it doesn't hurt to go through the steps to see if there are any unusual assembly sequences—some of these can be difficult to undo if done out of order, and on complex kits, these steps might not be readily apparent until it's too late to fix.

Prior to assembly, determine how you want the finished structure to look: How do you want to paint and weather it? What signs do you plan to add? Do you want to include interior details? Are additional roof or exterior details needed? Do you want to incorporate interior or exterior lighting?

Any of these factors will influence how you assemble the structure. As you'll see in chapter 5, interior details and lighting need to be planned ahead because, by the time you glue a roof in place, it's often too late to go back and add them later.

Wood kits require painting, which makes them seem more complex, but it's a good idea to approach all structure kits as requiring painting. Manufacturers today usually mold their plastic kits in, as they say, "appropriate colors," but unfortunately unpainted plastic—regardless of the color—almost always looks like unpainted plastic. A quick coat of paint will improve the appearance of any kit.

Before starting assembly, determine whether you need to paint individual parts before putting them together, whether you can partially assemble a kit and paint it in subassemblies, or if you can fully assemble it before painting. (Chapter 7 provides details on painting.)

13 Some wall joints have notches or ridges to keep walls in alignment. This is an outbuilding from a Walthers HO grain elevator kit.

14 Apply a bead of liquid plastic cement along the rear of the joint and hold the walls in place until the bond takes hold. If the joint doesn't stay aligned, clamp the pieces together.

15 With butt-joint walls, make sure the proper walls overlap. Wall ends may not be at a 90-degree angle, so check them by holding the walls against a square.

16 You can make a wall end square by rubbing it against a flat file held against a wood block.

Whenever I begin working on a structure, I find a box in which to keep all the parts for the kit. This can be the box the kit came in; however, kit boxes often are not big enough to hold completed subassemblies. Boxes with separate (or flip-up) lids work best. Since I often work on several projects at once, it is vital to keep all parts together for each project. This includes materials not included with the original kit—for example, interior details, figures, decals, printed signs, lighting components, and roof details. I also include any notes, such as paint colors (it's frustrating to return to a kit a few months after starting it and have no memory of what shade of dark red you painted the initial brickwork).

Prepping plastic kits

One reason styrene kits are popular is that plastic is easy to glue and work with. The injection-molding also nicely captures all kinds of texture, including brick walls, asphalt roofing, and wood grain.

Plastic kit parts are attached to sprues. In the molding process, plastic is forced into cavities in metal dies to form parts. Sprues are the paths the plastic travels, and gates are small extensions that ensure that the plastic travels completely through the die for each part.

It's a good idea to leave parts on their sprues until you actually need them because small pieces can easily become lost. Another reason is that parts are often labeled with numbers on the sprue, and since many kits have some parts that appear identical, leaving them in place can avoid confusion, **3**. A sprue can also serve as a convenient handle when painting parts, especially smaller ones.

Carefully remove parts from sprues as needed. Don't twist a part loose or simply pull it from the sprue. Doing so will often damage the part and leave a gap or bulge that is visible when the kit is assembled.

A hobby knife with a chisel-tip blade works well for removing parts, **4**. Depending upon the design and thickness of the sprue, you may be able to slice the part cleanly with little or no cleanup needed. If the space is tight, it's usually best to cut into the sprue a bit and then clean up the part once it's separated.

You can also remove parts with sprue cutters, which come in two types. Tweezer-style cutters work well for removing small parts, often with no cleanup necessary, **5**. Larger sprue cutters look like wire cutters, but they cut with a shearing action, **6**. They are especially effective on parts with heavy

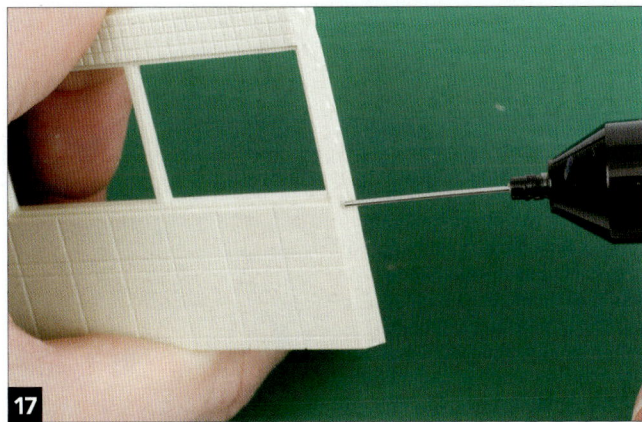

17 The alignment on this City Classics store kit was good, so I applied glue to the beveled edge of one wall.

18 Press the walls together, making sure that the joint is solid. Check that the alignment is good, in this case with tiles and panel seams matching between walls.

19 Right Clamps are designed to clamp two pieces at a 90-degree angle. They have gaps on the back that allow cement to be applied to the joint.

20 Bar clamps can be used to hold many types of joints, such as a front wall to a building base, as shown here, or walls to each other.

or large sprues and gates. However, you'll usually have to do some cleanup when using them.

Once the part is off the sprue, clean up the cutting marks if necessary. If the cutting mark is not in a visible location, such as the edge of a window frame behind a wall, there's no need to trim it as long as the part fits properly. If the part will be visible, you can remove the material in several ways. One method is to use a hobby knife to carefully trim the area, using a light touch and multiple passes, **7**. This is generally the quickest method and will leave a clean edge, but you need to use care as it's easy for the blade to wander into the piece and remove too much material.

You can also use a small file, emery board, or sanding stick, **8**. These tools may take longer, but there's less chance of damaging the part. You can also remove most of the material with a knife and then finish with a file or sanding stick. Make sure the sanding tool is at the proper angle to the part, and check your work frequently to make sure you're not removing too much material.

Make sure all visible flash is cleaned from parts. Flash is plastic overflow from the molding process that appears along part edges and on mold parting lines, **9**. You can usually remove it with a hobby knife, followed with a file or abrasive pad if needed.

At this point, you should determine how you will paint the various parts—individually or in subassemblies—and do any necessary painting before beginning assembly.

The exact progression of assembly steps varies from kit to kit, but even for large structures, the process usually involves putting together smaller subassemblies, and then combining the subassemblies. If a kit has separate window and door frames, it's usually a good idea to paint them and the walls separately before gluing them in place. Otherwise, generally follow the kit instructions.

Gluing plastic

Liquid plastic cement is usually the best choice for gluing plastic parts together. The cement effectively liquefies the mating surfaces and provides an extremely strong bond, formed by the plastic itself. Once the joint sets, it's usually impossible to separate the parts without damaging them.

Plastic cements are either a liquid or a gel. Liquid cements are thinner than water and include Testor's Plastic Cement (no. 3502) and Tamiya Extra Thin. Gel-type cements are thicker,

21 Micro-Mark's magnetic gluing jig works well for holding walls (or other parts) in alignment for gluing.

22 Rubber bands are another option for holding corner joints together, especially for tall structures.

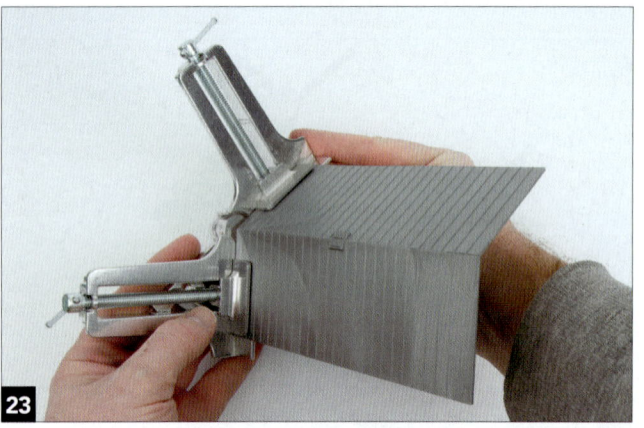
23 An adjustable corner clamp can hold walls, roof sections, or other parts at any angle. For longer pieces, you may need two clamps.

24 City Classics makes a set of plastic braces including inside and outside corners. They can be glued inside almost any plastic or wood structure.

which makes them easier to apply to certain locations. For gel, I use Testor's Liquid Cement for Plastic Models (no. 3507) and Model Master (no. 8872C), both of which come in 1-ounce bottles with needle-tip applicators. I prefer these cements over tube-type glues, which tend to be thicker and more difficult to apply precisely.

The type of glue you use depends on the type of joint. Use liquid cement if you can hold the joint tightly in place and apply the liquid with a brush from the back side of the joint, **10**. Many liquid cements include a brush inside the bottle top, but I find that these are often too large for precise applications. I keep a small paintbrush handy expressly for this purpose. (I marked it with a piece of tape near the end, so I won't accidentally use it for paint.)

While holding or clamping the joint, apply the liquid cement. Capillary action draws the cement into the joint. Hold the parts in place until the glue sets (usually just a few seconds). Let major joints, such as walls and roofs, cure for an hour or two before doing any additional work on them that will put stress on the joint.

For many joints, gel-type cement works well, **11**. Use the applicator to run a bead of cement on one of the parts, **12**. Press the parts together, making sure the alignment is correct, until the joint begins to hold.

With either type of cement, take care not to get any onto a visible surface, or it will mar the plastic. If this does happen, remove it immediately with a knife or toothpick (don't use a paper towel or tissue, as paper fibers will become imbedded in the plastic). If you don't notice the cement right away, wait until it cures, and then remove it as best you can with a knife or needle file and touch up the area with paint.

Wall joints
Corners where walls meet tend to be the trickiest joints, especially on tall structures. It can be difficult to keep long, narrow joints—which have very little surface area to glue—aligned and firmly held together while applying cement. Assembly techniques differ based on the size and type of joint. In general, start with joining two walls together, and then, for a four-wall structure, join the other two walls. Let the joints set until they are firm and then glue the remaining two joints, one at a time. Trying to glue two joints at once can be a challenge.

Manufacturers mold wall joints many different ways. The best ones have some type of interlocking notches that keep the walls in alignment, **13**. Others may have a vertical ridge on one or both wall edges to guide the parts, **14**. Some kits have walls with simple 45-degree angles. Others require a butt joint between walls.

25 Simply glue the corner brace inside the wall joint. Make sure both sides are glued to smooth wall areas with no protrusions, and that the braces won't be visible through windows.

26 Some structures, like this Walthers HO hobby shop, include a base. They can be helpful in keeping walls aligned, and also provide a floor for later supporting interior details.

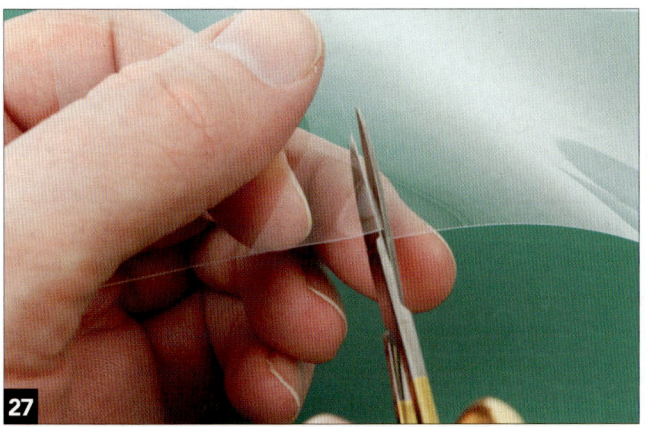

27 Scribe clear sheet styrene lightly to mark cutting lines. Then use a small scissors to cut the material to fit the window spaces.

28 Clear parts cement is white, but it dries clear and glossy. Apply it using the bottle tip or a toothpick.

Joining butt-jointed walls can be tricky. To start, make sure the proper wall overlaps the other. On some, buildings it will be obvious, as one wall will have brick texture on the end, but with others, it's not so easy. Making a mistake here can result in a problem that is difficult to fix when you get to the final joint.

Some kits have wall ends molded at a true 90-degree angle, but many have wall ends that angle slightly. This angle—called *draft*—is a by-product of engineering the part so it releases easily from its die. Test-fit the walls by holding them at a 90-degree angle (use a small square to make sure). You'll quickly see if the walls butt together firmly or if the mating edge is angled, **15**.

There are a couple of ways to square an angled wall. For small pieces, a NorthWest Short Line True Sander works well (see photo 12 in chapter 1). Use fairly coarse paper to start and fine paper for the final passes. Remove only as much material as needed and check the piece frequently.

You can also use a large file. It's difficult to get a perfect joint by freehanding it, so clamp or hold the file to a wood block with the file overhanging the edge, leaving a 90-degree angle, **16**. Rub the wall edge across the file, swapping ends after every few passes to even out the pressure on each end.

Another option for thin walls is to scrape the wall end with a hobby knife until it's square. Regardless of the method, check the joint frequently until the fit is tight, with no gap showing on the outside of the joint.

If one or both walls are warped, or if the joint can't be simply held in place with no gaps or other alignment problems, you'll need to clamp the walls in place. (More on that in a bit.) For small walls (especially thick ones), if you can hold the pieces in alignment with no gaps showing without applying any pressure, you can simply apply glue, **17**, hold the joint for a few seconds, and set the pieces aside until they set, **18**.

With some joints, you can provide more gluing area by adding a piece of square styrene strip to one wall before joining the sections together. Whether this is possible (as well as the size of the strip) is determined if any nearby windows, doors, or other details interfere.

With self-aligning wall joints, test-fit the mating walls. Again, if you can hold them in place with light pressure and they stay in alignment, apply glue and let them set, **14**. If not, you'll have to clamp them.

Walls with 45-degree bevels and no alignment notches or ridges are often the most difficult to align. As with

29 Carefully set the glazing in place. As here, one piece of glazing can fit over several window openings.

30 Hold the glazing in place while lightly touching a brush of liquid plastic cement to the edge. Continue holding the glazing gently for a few seconds until the bond takes hold.

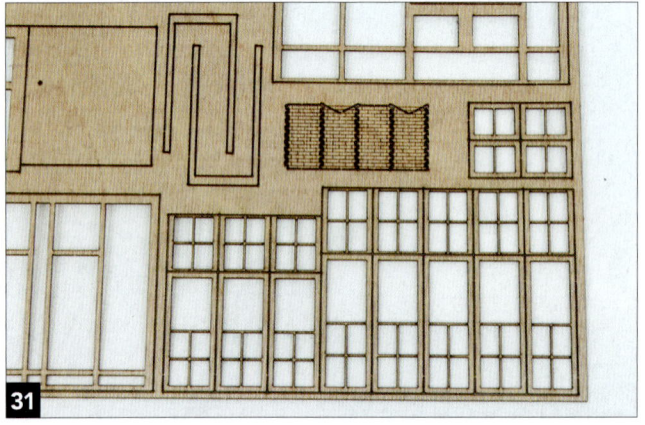
31 Laser-cutting is precise and provides very fine detail items, walls, doors, and individual window frame components.

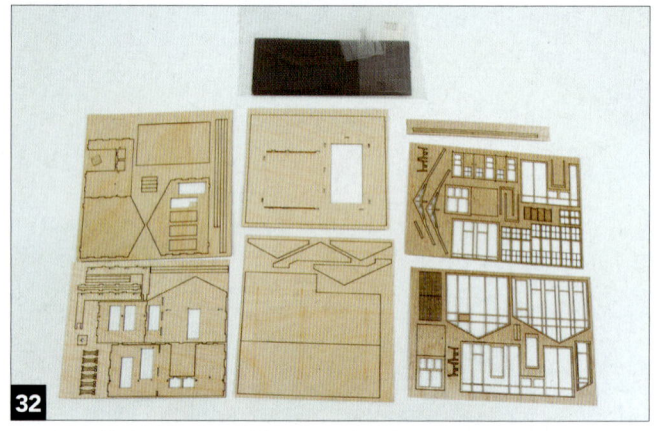
32 Lay out all the parts and become familiar with them. Even this small GC Laser depot kit has hundreds of laser-cut parts.

other walls, start by test-fitting them, cleaning the mating surfaces with a knife or file if needed. Clamping is usually the best way to join them; with some, you can add a square styrene reinforcing post as done with butt-jointed walls.

Clamping wall joints

There are several ways to clamp wall joints in place during assembly. Coffman Graphic Solutions makes the Right Clamp, a specialty clamp designed for joining materials at right angles, **19** (also see photo on page 5). These clamps are available in several sizes ranging from 1" to 7" jaw lengths. Small walls can be held with a single clamp, while longer joints might require one at each end.

Thumbscrews on the clamps allow you to adjust them for walls of varying thicknesses and details, such as those with building facades. The clamps have open areas on the backs, so you can easily apply glue.

Place the walls into the clamp. Get each wall into its approximate position while tightening the thumbscrews with light pressure. Work the walls into their final alignment and tighten the screws so the walls are firmly in place. Add liquid plastic cement to the rear of the joint with a brush and set the assembly aside to dry.

Right Clamps are suited for most walls, especially those with no alignment notches or ridges. However, they won't work well if the backs of the walls have protruding details.

You can also use small bar clamps, such as Quick-Grips, to hold butt-jointed walls and many other types of joints, **20**. Get the parts into position with light pressure and then add cement when the corner is in final alignment. These clamps work on butt joints as well as some joints with alignment pieces, or joints with protrusions on the rear pieces.

Gluing jigs can also be helpful for some wall joints. Micro-Mark's magnetic gluing jig (no. 60304) is a steel tray with 90-degree walls around it. You can use a combination of magnets and clamps to hold walls (or any other parts) in alignment for gluing, **21**.

Yet another option, especially for taller buildings or for getting the last of four joints into alignment, is using rubber bands. Place several of them around a structure until the joint is tight and aligned and then add cement, **22**.

Sometimes walls need to be joined at odd angles. This also happens often with roof pieces, when two halves of a roof must be joined at the roof cap. The best tool I've found for this task is an adjustable corner clamp, **23**. Multiple brands are available; the one

Because it is thinner than a hobby knife blade, a razor blade does a good job of cutting the fine wood frets that hold parts to the sheet.

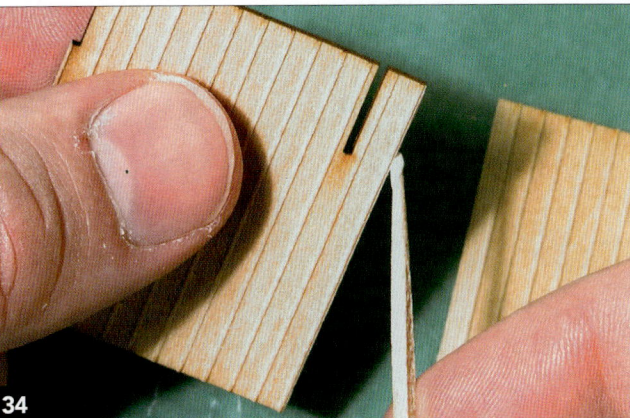
To fix this broken board-and-batten wall, I first spread white glue along the broken edge with a toothpick.

After butting the pieces together, I placed the wall flat on a piece of waxed paper. I then set weights on top to keep it flat.

Use a toothpick to add a bit of CA or white glue to a mating wall edge.

I use is called the Pony, and it's made (appropriately) by the Adjustable Clamp Co.

Once walls are together, corners can be reinforced if necessary. You can simply glue a piece of square styrene strip in place, or you can use City Classics plastic corner braces, **24** and **25**.

Bases and roofs

Many plastic kits include bases. You may or may not choose to use the base provided, depending upon how you plan to plant the finished building on your layout. In general, use the provided base if possible—it can be handy for keeping walls aligned during assembly and for adding interior details later, **26**.

Chapter 8 provides more details on planting structures into layouts, but a good rule of thumb is to make structures removable if possible to provide access for adding details and lighting, to clean structures and the layout, and to allow for later layout changes.

Roof assembly varies widely among kits. Many kits include detailed roofs with textures such as shingles, metal sheathing, and tarpaper seams. Structures with flat roofs usually have a single-piece roof, while peaked roofs often have two pieces. You can glue these together with an adjustable corner clamp as described earlier.

Before gluing a roof in place, decide whether you want to make the roof removable. Consider this if you have added interior lighting, or if you think you might later want to add interior details or lights.

For peaked roofs, if you've assembled the roof properly, it should sit in place without gluing. Likewise for flat roofs, if the walls have an interior ledge (ridges molded into the upper interior walls or separate support strips glued in place) and the roof fits properly, you shouldn't have to glue it.

Some kits supply plain styrene sheet for roofs. There are a few ways you can treat these, for example, to simulate a membrane, tarpaper, or gravel-covered roof. Turn to chapter 6 on exterior detailing for some ideas.

Windows, doors, and glazing

Some plastic kits have window and door frames molded into the walls; many others have separate frames that must be glued in place, **10**. For separate frames, be sure to paint them the proper trim color before adding them to the walls. For molded-in-place items, paint them before adding window glazing.

Frames can be glued in place before assembling the walls, unless doing so would interfere with clamping and securing wall corners.

Hold the joint securely for a few seconds. The interlocking tabs ensure good alignment between the walls. All the walls were painted on their parts sheets before assembly.

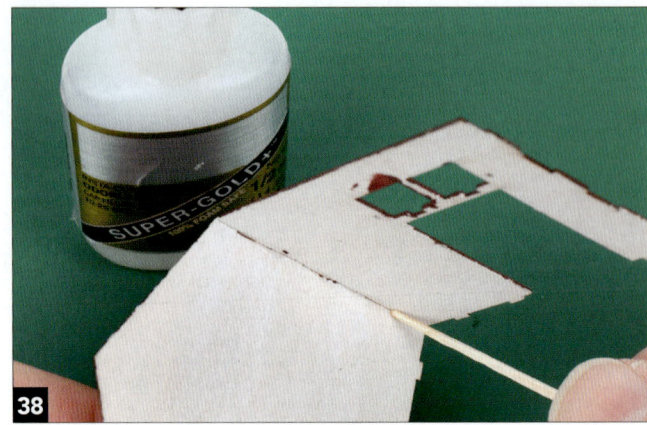

For added strength, add CA along the inside of the corner joint. This is usually sufficient for small structures.

Square stripwood can be used to reinforce corner joints and those between walls and floors, as on this large HO depot.

Glue the walls together in subassemblies and then glue the subassemblies together.

Window glazing (clear material) varies among kits and manufacturers. Some include injection-molded clear parts sized to fit behind each window. Others include clear sheets of thin clear styrene or acetate that must be cut to fit each window.

My preference is to use thin (.015") clear styrene sheet, available from Evergreen and others. Injection-molded glazing is thick, which is often apparent and sometimes has visible imperfections. I'm not a fan of acetate. It can't be glued with plastic cement, and its flexibility causes it to show creases and ripples more easily than clear styrene, especially on larger windows.

When working with clear styrene, first mark it by scribing it lightly by pulling a hobby knife backward, using a straightedge to ensure a straight line. Cut it with small scissors to ensure clean edges (the scribe-and-snap technique doesn't work well with clear plastic), **27**.

You have two options in gluing clear styrene (injection-molded or sheet) in place. The safest way is to use clear parts cement, such as Model Master, **28**. Use a toothpick or bottle applicator, depending on the spacing, to place the cement on the interior around the edge of the opening and then use tweezers or fingers to carefully set the glazing in place, **29**. If any cement gets on the surface, it will dry clear and glossy.

Glazing can often be cut so that one piece covers several window openings. Doing this is much easier than cutting individual pieces for each opening, and it allows the cement to be located away from the openings.

The other option is to use liquid plastic cement, applied with a brush. To do this, hold the glazing gently in place from behind. Touch a brush of cement to the edge of the glazing at each corner from behind, **30**. Capillary action will draw it into the joints, keeping it off of the window surface itself. Hold the glazing for a few seconds, while the cement takes hold, and then carefully let go. If you accidentally move the glazing so cement gets on the window surface, immediately pull the piece off, discard it, and try again.

Details and finishing

Continue adding details and other parts. Small components can be glued in place with either plastic cement (make sure you remove paint from mating surfaces) or cyanoacrylate adhesive (CA).

(You can see how the structures shown in this chapter were detailed in chapter 5. Chapter 7 shows methods of painting and finishing buildings, and chapter 9 shows how to blend finished models into scenes and scenery.)

Use CA to glue the completed structure assembly to the base, applying the glue from inside (and under the base on the wall tabs) to keep any stray glue hidden from view.

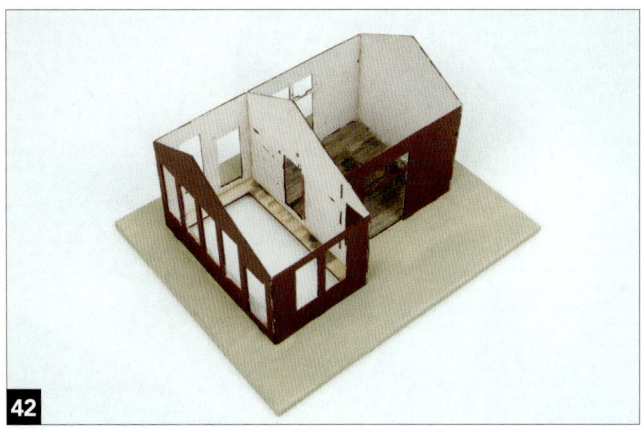
Before adding any interior details, I painted the base and stained the depot's floor.

I glued the large trim sections in place with matte medium, adding it with a toothpick. Matte medium works well as a glue and dries clear and flat.

Make sure the trim piece is aligned properly. Using tweezers, I placed it carefully at the base of the wall and leaned it up into position.

Wood kits

Assembling a wood structure kit isn't much more difficult than assembling a plastic kit, but some different techniques, tools, and adhesives come into play. Compared to plastic, which is nonporous, relatively strong, and unaffected by moisture, wood parts—especially thin walls and components—can warp and expand when painted, and break if not handled carefully.

Most wood kits these days, such as the depot in photo **1**, have parts laser-cut from sheets of thin wood or plywood, including window and door openings in walls, window frames, and small detail parts, **31**. Laser-cutting permits extremely tight tolerances, allowing precise alignment of parts, and kit components generally fit together quite well.

Traditional wood kits are still available. These—called craftsman kits for a reason—require modelers to do a lot of cutting of stripwood pieces, sometimes require modelers to cut larger pieces (such as walls) to shape, or require cutting window openings. Otherwise, construction steps and techniques are similar to those shown here for laser-cut kits.

Preparation

As with a plastic kit, the first step in preparing a wood kit is to take inventory, **32**. Make sure all parts are there and become familiar with all of them. With wood kits, do as much painting as possible prior to assembly—especially with trim pieces of various colors. As chapter 7 shows, paint these pieces while still on their frets if possible. Painting both sides of all pieces minimizes warping of the wood. Most of the photos here show an HO depot kit from GC Laser, but the steps are similar for other wood kits.

Leave parts on their frets until you need them. Don't try to pop parts from their sheets by pressing them with your fingers—cut the frets to release them. You can use a hobby knife, but hobby blades are often wider than the laser-cut gap. A single-edge razor blade is thinner, extremely sharp, and works well for this, **33**.

Many laser-cut kits include interior wood flooring and a wood base. As with plastic models, determine how you want to treat these, and decide whether you want to add interior details prior to starting assembly.

If a part breaks, it's a simple repair, **34**. Place a piece of waxed paper on a flat surface. Apply white glue to the broken edge, butt the pieces together, and place them on the waxed paper with a weight on top, **35**.

45 I pressed it into place until it set. If any glue gets on the surface, you can wipe it off and then touch up the area with paint.

46 Apply clear parts adhesive to the rear of the frame with a toothpick.

47 Then carefully set the laser-cut clear styrene glazing in place, keeping the outside edges aligned.

48 Set the windows in place, then apply matte medium or white glue with a toothpick around the frame edges to secure them.

Whenever possible, paint all the parts while they're still on their sheets. You can use a brush or an airbrush for this. Paint both sides to minimize warping—you can use common latex primer for the rear sides of walls.

Joining walls and components

Medium-viscosity CA is usually my choice of adhesive for assembling wood kits, as it penetrates the wood to bond joints strongly and quickly. You can use white glue or wood glue, but you'll need to hold joints in place longer, and the joint will take longer to cure, which can be a challenge for long seams.

Test-fit each joint. Wall sections in laser-cut kits often interlock, making assembly relatively foolproof. Use a toothpick to apply small dabs of glue to one mating edge and then press the pieces together and hold for a few seconds, **36** and **37**. Once it sets, you can add a thin bead of CA behind the joint to reinforce it, **38**.

For long joints (on many O scale buildings and two-story or taller structures in HO), you may want to add square stripwood behind the corner to strengthen it (⅛" is usually sufficient), **39**. Keep in mind where interiors will be visible through windows or open doors.

Keep adding walls in subassemblies until the entire building is together, **40**. After the building is together, you can glue the structure to its base, **41**. For the depot shown here, I first painted the base and stained the interior floor, **42**. I'll add an interior to the building later.

Keep adding parts to the building shell. Test-fit everything before adding glue. When adding thin trim sheets, be very careful with glue. I used a toothpick to add small dabs of matte medium on the back of the material so that any glue that became visible would dry clear and flat, **43**. I then carefully pressed the trim, which was painted before installation, in place, **44** and **45**.

If a bit of glue gets on the surface, wipe it off quickly with the end of a toothpick if you can, and then touch up the area with paint if it's still visible when the structure is complete.

Windows

The window detail in laser-cut kits is generally very good. Most kits include separate pieces for the upper and lower sashes and for the frames.

Some manufacturers use peel-and-stick adhesive on the rear of window pieces. This makes it easy to align and fasten glazing to the frames with no mess. On other kits, such as this one, you have to glue the glazing

Glue a lower sash in a raised position if you want to show one or more windows open.

The roof itself is a sturdy subassembly that fits over the structure walls without any need for gluing.

Guidelines help keep the simulated rolled roofing material parallel with the roof edges. A thin coat of white glue holds the paper material in place.

A bit of black paint simulates tarred seams between sections of roofing material.

in place, **46**. To do so, dab a small amount of clear parts adhesive on the rear of the frame with a toothpick, and then carefully set the glazing in place, using your fingers to keep them aligned, **47**.

Don't use CA for this, as the vapors from the glue will cause frosting or crazing on the clear styrene glazing.

Glue the windows in place, using white glue or matte medium from inside the structure, **48**. If your kit includes separate upper and lower sashes, you can position one or more windows in an open position, **49**.

Roof and details
Many laser-cut kit roofs are designed for a press or placement fit, allowing them to be easily removed, **50**. Typical construction is adding wood roof panels over laser-cut angle pieces, which match the shape and slope of the tops of the walls.

Roofing materials vary. This kit included dark gray paper that represents rolled tarpaper roofing. Following the instructions, I installed it from the bottom of the roof upward by applying a thin coat of white glue and then pressing the material in place, **51**. I finished it by adding the chimney and painting simulated tarred seams with black paint and a brush, **52**.

Other materials
As you gain experience, you may come across structure kits made from other materials, notably resin and plaster.

Resin components, at first glance, look much like injection-molded styrene. The major difference when assembling is that plastic solvent cements will not work on resin—resin must be glued with either CA or epoxy.

Because resin parts are often coated with a mold-release compound, a good first step is to scrub them in warm water with liquid dish detergent (such as Dawn) and a toothbrush. This helps adhesion for both paint and glue during construction.

Resin can be filed and sanded much like plastic, but be aware that the resulting dust can be a major respiratory irritant—wear a dust mask and work in a well-ventilated area.

Plaster walls and components can be sanded, carved, and shaped with knives, files, and sandpaper. White glue works well for gluing plaster parts together. Because plaster is a porous material, painting it requires some special techniques (see chapter 7 for some tips).

1

CHAPTER THREE

Modular and kitbashed structures

May Brothers is an HO scale building made from modular wall sections from DPM (Woodland Scenics). Several companies offer modular components in a variety of window and door arrangements and wall styles. The building at right is a photo print glued to the backdrop.

Sometimes the building you want to model just isn't available commercially. Before deciding to scratchbuild a structure, consider using modular components, which can be built in any number of arrangements, **1**. You could also kitbash the structure—taking parts from one kit and altering them or combining them with parts from other kits to create a new building, **2**.

Kitbashing is the technique of rearranging components from one or more kits to create a completely different structure. The late Art Curren kitbashed elements of this industrial complex on Kalmbach's HO Milwaukee, Racine & Troy club layout.

Modular structures

Modular components offer flexibility in creating structures. Several companies offer modular components. Brick walls of various designs are made by Woodland Scenics (DPM) in N and HO and Lunde Studios (HO), **3**. Walthers offered brick modular walls in HO and N, and although the line has been discontinued, you can still track them down online. Great West Models sells HO modular walls representing modern prefab concrete structures, and Bar Mills offers modular laser-cut wood kits in HO scale. Most of these include wall sections with various window arrangements, corner trim, cornices, pilasters, and other details.

I wanted a large, low-relief building for a 1960s HO scene I was working on. The building would be rail-served by a spur track at the edge of the street. It had to be fairly imposing—two or three stories tall and long enough to park a couple of boxcars (and large enough to logically warrant rail traffic). It also had to be narrow, as I only had a few inches between the street and rail spur and the backdrop.

I decided to make the business a grocery wholesaler. This would allow incoming rail loads to arrive in a variety of boxcars and refrigerator cars. I also wanted to include some basic interior detail, as well as lighting—many areas like this were switched at night, and lighting always adds interest.

I couldn't find a commercial kit that matched what I needed, but DPM's brick modular wall sections had the basic appearance that I was looking for. I'll walk through the steps I used for building this structure, as well as the basic techniques that apply to other modular buildings (and kitbashing).

Start by laying out the sections for the walls. You can photocopy the wall sections and use the copies as an aid. You can also scan the wall sections and use Adobe Photoshop or another graphics program to lay out potential walls and structures. Either way, play with various arrangements until you find one that works.

Some quick sketching and measuring led me to design a building that was seven wall sections long and three sections (four stories) tall, giving me a scale 143-foot-long, 63-foot-tall building. I made it one section deep, so including a loading dock, the building measured just over 3" from the backdrop to the front of the loading dock.

I used three large door sections along the loading dock, with combination door and window pieces at one corner to represent an office. Making the entire wall plain brick would have been rather dull, so I mixed in several two-window sections as well, with a plan of bricking over several of these openings, as was done on many similar prototype structures.

Wall construction

DPM modular kits include wall sections and the vertical pilasters that run between each section—these serve to reinforce and hide the vertical joints. Kits also include the top (cap) sections, as well as components for a loading dock.

3 DPM's modular components include wall sections with various door and window arrangements and trim pieces.

4 To simulate a bricked-over window, cut a piece of brick sheet slightly larger than the opening. File the piece until it's a press-fit, and then add liquid plastic cement from the back.

5 Keep wall sections square with a jig and a square (here, a drafting triangle), or by clamping a straightedge to a board or workbench.

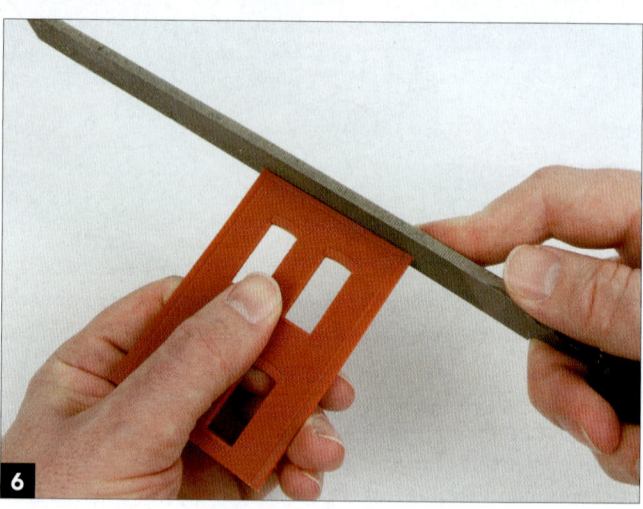

6 Make sure mating edges are smooth and square to ensure a solid joint both structurally and visually.

If you want to modify any of the wall sections, do so before starting construction. I waited to brick over the window openings until my structure was assembled, which made the process more difficult.

You can use any brick sheet to do this. In my scrapbox, I found part of a brick wall from a long-ago modified kit. I liked that its style of brick was different than the DPM wall. When placed in the opening, it gave the appearance that it was done some time after the structure was built.

Measure a window opening and cut the brick sheet to fit, **4**. Cutting the piece slightly larger than needed and then filing it to size results in a snug press-fit. Touch a brush of liquid plastic cement to the joint at the rear of the wall to secure it.

Keeping walls square is extremely important, and it's a challenge when building large modular structures or kitbashed buildings in which each wall comprises multiple sections, **5**. A temporary or permanent jig with right-angle stops helps—I used Micro-Mark's no. 60304 gluing jig and a drafting square for initial assemblies, and a large straightedge clamped to my workbench for wider assemblies.

Make sure the top and bottom of each section is square and smooth, **6**. With DPM modules, nothing covers the horizontal seams, so they must be tight fitting. Use a file or a True Sander to do this (shown in chapter 2). Test-fit the joint between two sections until it is snug and without gaps.

A backing piece is optional, but it will result in a stronger joint, **7**. Cut a narrow strip of .005" sheet styrene and glue it to the rear of one wall at the joint. Apply a bead of gel-type plastic cement along both the backing strip and the joint edge and then press the mating section in place. Do this over a metal surface, such as the jig, or over a piece of waxed paper so that the sections don't stick to your work surface.

You can do without a backing piece, but you'll need to allow more time for the joint to set before handling the piece. With a backing piece, you can usually move on within a few minutes.

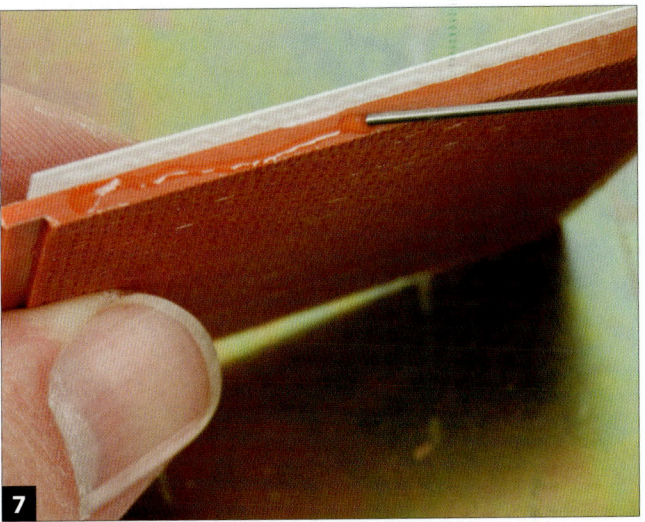

A thin backing of sheet styrene helps reinforce the horizontal joints between wall sections.

Glue pilasters to one mating edge of each wall section. The pilasters provide an overlapped joint that is quite strong.

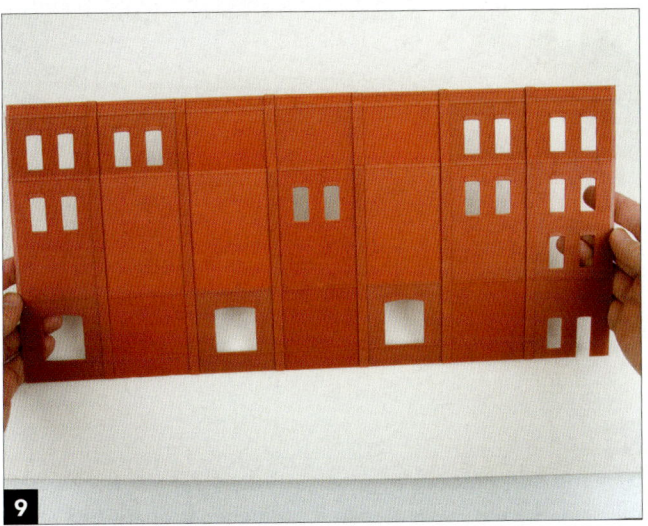

Glue the wall sections together to form the entire wall, making sure each joint is square as you go.

Clamp the corner securely together and then add liquid plastic cement to the rear of the corner seams.

Glue styrene strips inside the walls to support the roof. Then add glue to the supporting strips to hold the roof.

As the roof was foam core, I used foam-safe cyanoacrylate adhesive (CA) and then pressed the roof in place.

13 Use CA to fill gaps at the corners and along the roof seam. Then use accelerator to cure it.

14 To clean up the CA, you can use a file or a hobby knife to shape it.

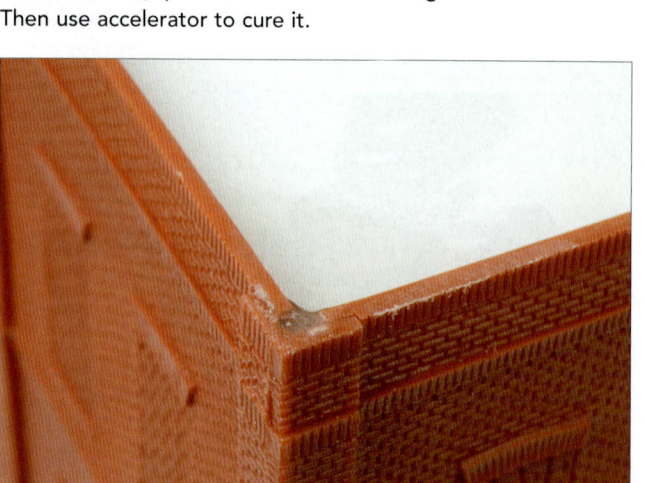
15 Finished joints, seams, and filled areas should have no gaps. Reapply CA if needed.

16 Glue the dock sections together, and then glue the dock to the building. Styrene spacers keep it positioned properly and also add strength.

Make sure the wall edges align. For the DPM walls, the actual outside edges aren't critical, as they don't actually abut the neighboring piece; pilasters cover the joint and provide the gluing surface. Assemble each vertical section this way, checking that they're square as you go.

Add the pilasters to one edge of each of the vertical sections, **8**. Be sure to use the proper piece, as the kits include two types, and one is narrower for use on the corners. You can then glue the vertical sections to each other, **9**. Again, use a square to ensure that the pieces are aligned properly, and test-fit them before gluing. Add glue and press the pilasters firmly in place. Do this for each of the walls.

Glue the corner pilaster pieces together to form an L. Make sure you sand or file the mating edges to a 90-degree angle, as the DPM pieces have a slight taper to the edges. Glue this L to one wall of the corner. Once the cement has set, clamp the other wall in place and add liquid plastic cement to the end and rear of the joint with a brush, **10**.

Once the glue was set, I added City Classics corner reinforcing angles in a few places (see photo 25 on page 19). These add a great deal of strength, which is important for constructing large structures such as this one. Make sure they won't interfere with window frames or interior details.

Roof and loading dock
The roof can be made from almost any rigid sheet material. I had a large scrap piece of foam core handy, so I cut it to fit (sheet styrene also works well). For a flat roof, glue supporting strips of styrene around the inside edges of the walls, **11**. Strip size isn't critical—it just needs to be wide enough to support the roof. I ran a bead of foam-safe cyanoacrylate adhesive (CA) around the supports and pressed the foam core in place, **12**.

Fill any visible gaps on the roof at the corners, between wall sections, and between the roof and walls with CA. For large gaps, such as the corner seen in photo **13**, apply the CA in several layers, fixing it with CA accelerator after each layer. (I find this works better than plastic putty.) Then use a file and/or hobby knife to shape and clean up the CA, **14** and **15**. I

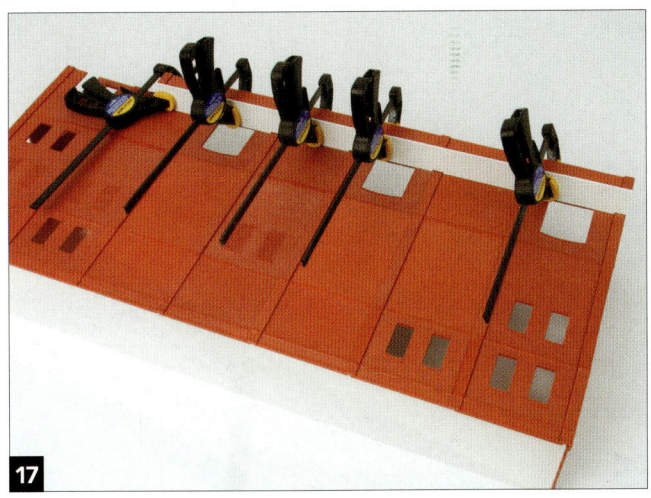

The dock deck is .080" styrene. I clamped it to get it to fit tightly to the base and glued it with liquid plastic cement from under the deck.

The loading dock doors are pieces of Evergreen corrugated styrene, painted a buff color, with black strip added as a gasket at the bottom.

Drill mounting holes for the canopy support rods. I used a piece of plastic cut at an angle as a guide for the slope.

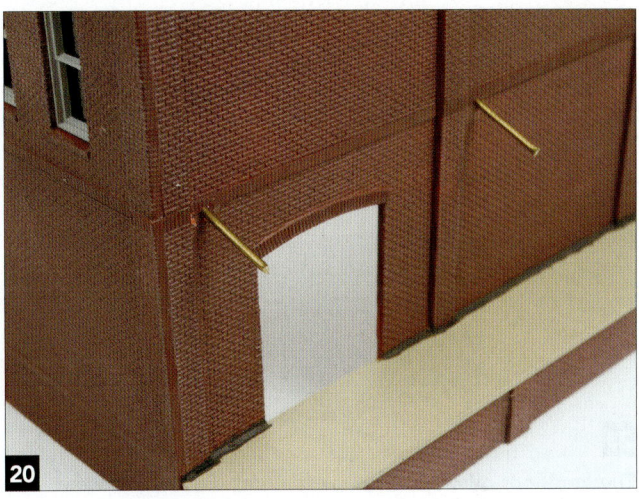

The canopy support rods should be shorter than the width of the canopy itself. The rods are glued in place with CA.

simply painted the roof grimy black to represent tarred roofing and then added several vents from Walthers no. 933-3733 roof detail set.

I wanted the loading dock to extend from the left end of the wall to the middle of the section next to the office on the right. I cut and fit a bit more than five DPM dock sections together. Glue several styrene spacers to the rear of the dock's brick facing to keep it the proper distance from the main wall, **16**. Use liquid plastic cement to glue it in place. The deck of the loading dock is thick sheet styrene (.080") cut to fit. Set it in place, mark the pilaster locations, and notch the styrene so it fits around them. Glue the deck in place with plastic cement, **17**. I had to clamp it to get a tight fit.

For the steps, I used a metal casting from a DPM kit I had in my shop. You can easily make steps by stacking thick sheet styrene. (See the scratchbuilt branch house in chapter 4 for details.)

Painting, decals, and windows

You can paint brick almost any shade of medium red to dark red or brown. I used Polly Scale boxcar red, applied with a wide brush. Be thorough, making sure the paint gets into all the mortar joints, seams, and pilasters. As explained in chapter 6, you can simulate brick mortar in many ways. I gave the whole building a thinned wash of light gray, cut a bit with the structure color (about 20 parts water or airbrush thinner, 2 parts gray, and 1 part boxcar red), and applied it with a wide, soft brush.

The large sign on the side is a decal that I designed using Photoshop Elements (as shown in chapter 7). I printed it on white decal paper and then cut it into strips to match the spaces between and atop the pilasters.

The door and window frames are separate pieces. I airbrushed them medium gray and then scraped the paint off of the inner mating surface of each. After pressing each frame in place in the opening, I touched a brush of liquid plastic cement to the seam from the back.

The loading dock is a mix of aged concrete and light gray, applied with a brush.

I wanted to have two of the freight dock doors open to allow for some interior details, and the DPM doors aren't suited for this. I made new

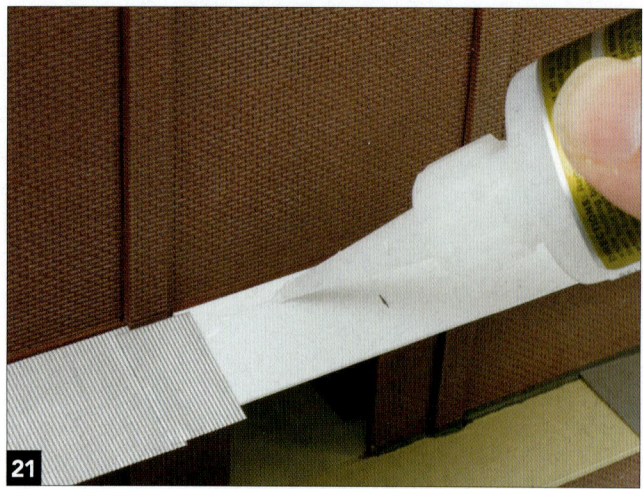
Glue the styrene canopy in place, and then use CA to secure Campbell corrugated aluminum sheet atop the styrene.

Paint the corrugated aluminum flat silver, then weather it by streaking various dark rust colors along the corrugations.

The first-floor office shadowbox features details, while the upper floor has just a hallway with walls and doors.

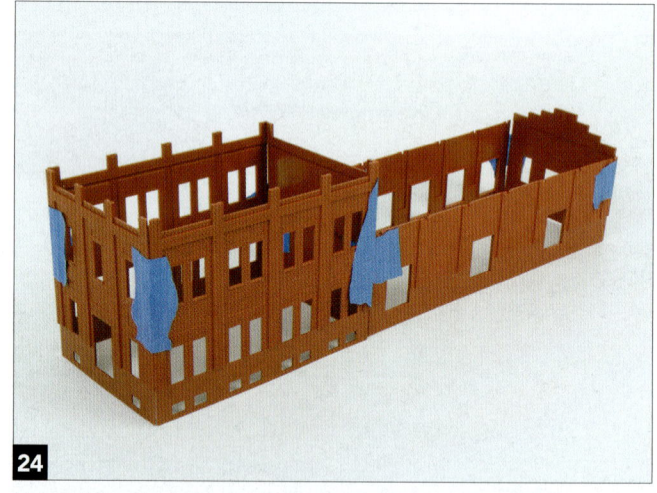
Here's how the basic Walthers brick freight house kit is intended: a two-story building with a one-story extension.

doors with small pieces of Evergreen corrugated styrene to represent roll-up style doors, **18**. I painted these a buff color, added a thin strip of black styrene at the bottom to represent a gasket, and glued them in place behind the openings. I glued one in the closed position and the other two open so just the bottoms are visible.

The loading dock needed a canopy. I wanted one covered with galvanized metal, which was typical for the era. Canopies are usually sloped to shed moisture. I started by adding 1/16" brass rod supports along the wall. To capture the slope, I used a piece of plastic cut to a slight angle as a guide for the bit in a pin vise, **19**. Making sure the holes were evenly spaced, I added six wires along the length of the dock, **20**. The wires extended a scale 12" shorter than the width of the dock. I used CA to glue the wires in place.

The canopy is a piece of .040" styrene cut to fit. The overhang stretches beyond the ends of the support wires but just shy of the edge of the loading dock so it won't interfere with rail cars on the siding. Use CA to secure it to the support rods, **21**.

I used Campbell corrugated aluminum sheet to represent galvanized metal. I cut it so that it would overhang the styrene canopy by a scale 6" or so. You can cut the corrugated sheet into scale 4-foot-wide pieces, or you can cheat a bit (as I did) and use wider pieces. You'll have to notch some pieces to fit around the pilasters. I used CA, but I'd recommend E6000 or Gorilla Glue instead, as the CA doesn't always stick well to the aluminum.

I painted the aluminum with a coat of flat silver (Polly Scale Flat Aluminum), **22**. I followed this with a combination of washes and drybrushing to streak several dark rust colors (roof brown, rail brown) down the corrugations to vary the appearance.

Interior details and lighting

Interior detailing doesn't have to be extensive to be effective. My goals for this building were to provide enough details to make it look like an active, busy place, and to make the details appropriate for a grocery wholesaler. (Chapter 5 goes into detail about how I added interior details and lights.)

I made extensive use of photographs, resizing them and printing them, to represent interior details. Behind the

25 The building could be stretched along a backdrop in a couple of ways. Here, I kept the two-story building as intended and doubled the length of the one-story section.

26 Another way to stretch the building is moving all of the back walls to the front and doubling the length of the entire building..

27 The kit could be converted to a larger, squarish industrial complex, but at least one additional kit would be needed to provide enough wall sections.

28 Two of the kit's two-story structures will eventually become a school building. If the rear wall of a structure won't be seen, it can simply be replaced by a plain sheet of styrene.

warehouse doors, I used photos of various grocery boxes and cases from the 1950s and '60s, reduced to the proper size. Some are simply glued flat to the backs of the shadowboxes, while others are glued to blocks for a 3-D appearance. I also added a couple of Preiser figures, making them visible through the openings.

The office shadowbox includes details from Preiser and Pola as well as figures and printed graphics, **23**. I also included a second floor, which is visible through the windows.

For the upper windows on the walls, I simply glued flat photos of stacks of cases to black mat board. I positioned these flats about an inch behind the windows and glued them in place on styrene spacers.

I used clear Christmas tree bulbs to light the warehouse area and office. A simple on-off slide or toggle switch can be added to the layout fascia or control panel to turn the lights on and off.

I blended the structure into the backdrop with a mix of building flats and graphics on the backdrop. (Chapter 9 provides details on how to do this.)

Kitbash planning

Once you've assembled a few kits and tackled a modular building, you're more than ready to kitbash a structure. The key is to look beyond the photo on a kit box—and ignore the name of the kit or what it's supposed to represent—and focus in a kit's features: the wall style and material, window and door placements, roofing material and style, and so on.

As an example, I started with a Walthers HO Water Street Freight Terminal kit (no. 933-3009). As designed, this is a typical freight house design, with a two-story, flat-roof section on one end, and a peaked-roof, single-story extension with multiple loading doors. You can see the intended basic kit in photo **24**.

Start by playing with the components. Masking tape works well for temporarily holding pieces together. You can photocopy walls and other parts, cut them apart, and tape them together. You can also scan the walls and rearrange them in a graphics program.

I thought this kit might work by converting it to a low-relief structure

David Popp kitbashed this paper mill complex on Kalmbach's HO club layout using a variety of kits, including several Walthers Lakeville warehouses, a Pikestuff engine house, a Walthers Magic Pan Bakeries, and Kibri tanks.

Jim Hediger rearranged walls from several Walthers machine shop kits to create this appliance factory. The Rix tank at left helps hide the rear structure joint with the backdrop.

along a backdrop to go with my modular building, so I tried two versions: leaving the two-story building as-is and doubling the length of the one-story section, **25**, and moving the rear wall to the front of each section and doubling the length of the entire building, **26**.

I also played around with making the building a more square industrial-type free-standing structure, although at least one more kit would be needed for this version, **27**. The last version I toyed with—and one that I may proceed with—is converting just the two-story section of it into a school, **28**. In playing with the wall sections, I found it strongly resembled the old high school building in my hometown, in selectively compressed size. But that's a project for another day.

The point is that any one kit can serve as the starting point for several different styles of structures, **29** and **30**.

This chapter can only provide an introduction to the subject of kitbashing. For more in-depth information, take a look at *How to Kitbash Structures* by Tony Koester (Kalmbach, 2013) and *Structure Projects for Your Model Railroad* (Kalmbach, 2014).

Kitbashing construction tips

Use a utility knife to cut kit walls. Make several light passes instead of fewer heavy passes.

Any butt-jointed wall joints must be as square as possible to hide the joint. A True-Sander does a nice job of providing clean edges.

As with modular structures, back wall joints with a piece of thin styrene to strengthen the joint.

When modifying buildings, you'll find yourself having to cut walls and other components. For thick walls, a razor saw or utility knife works better than a hobby knife—use a straightedge as a guide, and try to cut walls at a wall feature, such as a pilaster or post.

Be sure corners and mating edges are square before trying to join them. Reinforce joints with small backing pieces of thin sheet styrene, and reinforce corners as well.

Structures can also be modified by changing roofing and wall material: replacing shakes with shingles, adding rolled roofing over existing roofing, or laying corrugated metal siding or roofing over existing walls.

Roofs of many kitbashed buildings, such as the potential modifications shown in photos **25–27**, usually require substantial modification. It's often easiest to discard the kit's roof sections and start over with commercial roofing material.

Chapter 4 provides ideas for scratchbuilding materials and techniques that will also work for kitbashing.

CHAPTER FOUR

Scratchbuilding

Scratchbuilding is the process of creating a model from raw materials and components—building it from scratch, **1**. Scratchbuilding is often the best way to re-create specific prototype structures, as even the tremendous quantity of available kits doesn't even begin to approach the number of structures out there in real life, **2**. Many modelers shy away from scratchbuilding, but with the variety of available materials, building a structure from scratch can be as easy as building a kit.

You can scratchbuild a model to represent almost any prototype building. This HO structure, built from a Plexiglas core with styrene and textured brick overlays, represents a Swift & Co. branch house that served Caldwell, Idaho (see page 36).

This 1941 photo of Swift's Caldwell, Idaho, branch house was the inspiration for my HO scale model. I didn't try to create an exact copy; instead, I wanted to capture the overall flavor of the real thing. *Library of Congress*

Raw materials

Let's look at the raw materials, starting with plain sheet and strip material, **3**. Plain plastic and wood sheets are great for basic structure shells, walls, bases, and roofs. My first choice is usually styrene:

- It's inexpensive
- It's easy to cut, shape, and glue
- It's dimensionally stable
- It's unaffected by temperature and humidity

Sheet styrene is made in thicknesses from .005" to .125" (and even thicker), with .010", .020", .040", and .060" sheets especially handy. Clear styrene (usually .005" and .015") is generally my first option for window glazing.

You'll find strip styrene useful for many purposes, including interior bracing, window frames, trim, railings, molding, wall caps, and other details. It's typically sold in packages and usually sized in thousandths of an inch (such as .020" x .040"), but in some cases, it is available by prototype dimensions, such as HO scale 4 x 6.

Evergreen and Plastruct are brands readily available in hobby shops or online. If you're working on large projects, and you live in or near a large metro area, I highly recommend finding a plastics wholesaler (check the Yellow Pages or online) as a source. You can get styrene in various colors and other types of plastic in sheets up to 4 x 8 feet. Many wholesalers also offer cutoffs and scraps, which are larger than hobby sheets, at very reasonable prices, **4**.

Clear acrylic sheet, such as Plexiglas, is also handy for modeling, forming structure shells and bases, and other uses. It's heavier (generally .100") and thicker than styrene, and very strong—especially effective for large walls. In addition to clear, it's also made in white, translucent gray, and black.

Strip and sheet wood is also available in a variety of sizes and thicknesses, **5**. Unlike styrene, wood is affected by moisture and humidity. It can warp when painted or stained, and the grain can show through paint. Its greatest asset is its appearance—nothing looks more like wood than real wood. It takes stain well and has a naturally varied look.

3 Styrene is a versatile modeling material. It's available in sheets and strips in various dimensions and sizes.

4 I bought these Plexiglas acrylic sheets and .125" styrene sheet cutoffs from a local plastics dealer. The total cost was less than $10, and they provided raw materials for several projects.

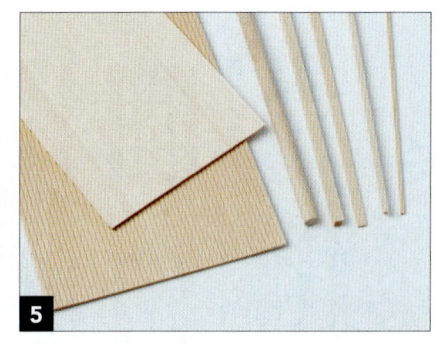

5 Balsa and basswood are both available in sheet and strip form in many dimensions.

6 Textured sheets include brick, concrete block, clapboard, shingles, and other simulated materials.

7 Structural shapes include plastic channels and beams as well as metal tubing and wire.

Balsa and basswood are the two most common types of wood used for modeling. Balsa is lightweight, soft, and easy to cut, with more grain. Basswood is hard, with a very tight grain. Thin plywood is also available. Manufacturers include Kappler, Midwest Products, and Northeastern.

You'll find many uses for both wood and plastic. My general guideline is that if I'm trying to represent wood itself (raw or weathered), then I use wood; otherwise, I use styrene.

Textured materials

Prototype structures are built with various types of distinctive siding materials. Wood siding includes clapboard (overlapping horizontal boards), board-and-batten (vertical planks with vertical thin caps, or battens, at the seams), tongue-and-groove (planks with grooves and protrusions on the edge that fit together), or simply planks butted together.

Brick gained popularity in the late 1800s and remained the most popular choice for permanent structures such as industrial buildings and stores well into the 1900s. Although we often think of brick as red, brick is made in many colors (from cream and buff to light red, dark red, and brown), sizes, and textures, and it can also be painted.

Other common building materials are stucco, concrete block, formed concrete, porcelain tile panels, corrugated iron (and other metal) sheets, prefab steel panels, and textured tin sheet. And these materials feature variations, including the different sizes and colors of blocks or the multiple spacing of siding. Modern buildings often feature steel-frame construction with wall panels of varied materials including large glass panels, polished metal, brick, concrete, and block.

Roofing is another category. Many types of shingles are used. Into the 1900s, common roofing included wood shakes, slate shingles (often featuring a diagonal pattern), and rolled tarpaper. In the mid-1900s, asphalt shingles—in a variety of shapes and colors—became common, and industrial buildings used corrugated metal, asphalt, membrane roofing, and roofing covered by pea gravel.

Scale representations of most of these materials are available in HO, N, and other scales, mainly in the form of textured styrene and wood sheets, **6**. Manufacturers include Bar Mills Models, Brawa, B.T.S., Evergreen, N Scale Architect, Pikestuff, Plastruct, and Walthers.

Structural shapes are another type of raw material. These include styrene

8 Numerous styles of doors and windows are made by Grandt Line, Campbell, Scale Structures Ltd., and others.

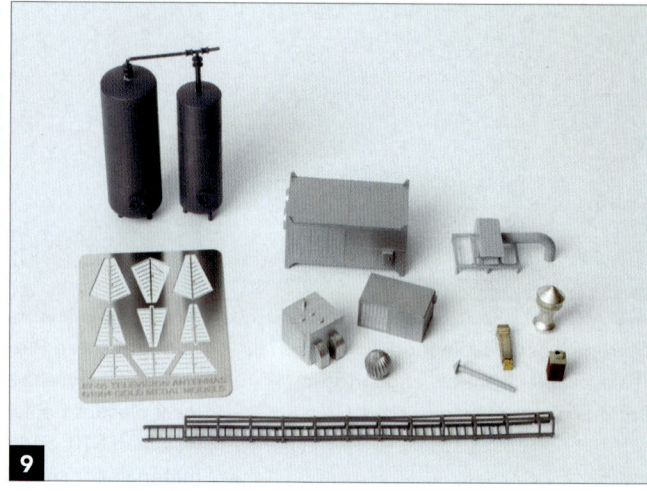

9 Many after-market structure details are available, including roof vents and chimneys, a/c units, ladders, staircases, railings, window awnings, tanks, and piping.

strips representing I beams, C channels, and Ls, as well as laced girders, and tubing and rod material, **7**. Evergreen and Plastruct both offer a variety of these materials.

When strength is critical, you'll also find many uses for metal tubing (round and square), rod, wire, and channels and other shapes. These are available from Detail Associates, K&S Engineering, Special Shapes, and others.

Windows, doors, and details

Windows and doors are often the most time-consuming, intricate parts to model on a scratchbuilt structure. Fortunately a wide variety of plastic and metal castings and laser-cut wood windows and doors are available from Alexander Scale Models (Tomar), American Model Builders, Bar Mills, Campbell, Grandt Line, Kitwood Hill Models, Monster Modelworks, Northeastern, Pikestuff, Rusty Stumps Scale Models, and Scale Structures Ltd., **8**. By looking through catalogs and websites, you can often find components that match or come close, saving you the trouble of building them yourself.

Many other details can also aid you in scratchbuilding. Roof details include chimneys, vents, cooling units, smokestacks, and antennae from City Classics, Gold Medal Models, Walthers, and many of the companies mentioned earlier, **9**. Other details include stairways, ladders, railings, awnings, canopies, tanks, exhaust fans, window air conditioners, and piping.

You might have to do some searching to find exactly what you're looking for. Along with Walthers and individual company websites, be sure to check eBay and other online sources, even if something is out of production (or if the company is no longer in business). If it's ever been made, it's likely still available somewhere.

You can also raid other kits for window frames, details, and other parts. Never throw away any leftover kit parts. Always keep a scrapbox of leftover parts from projects—you never know when you might need an item for a scratchbuilding or detailing project.

Planning

You can go to many sources for structure plans and information. Scale drawings are the best source. *Model Railroader* and other modeling magazines have published thousands of drawings of depots, towers, and industrial structures, and publishers have also compiled books of drawings, **10**. Railroad historical societies often publish drawings or offer for sale scale drawings or books of scale drawings from railroad blueprints.

If a structure still exists, being able to take photos and/or measure the building and make your own drawings is a huge advantage. When taking photos, back up, fill the frame, and stay as square to the wall as possible. Obviously, many industrial and other structures are off limits behind fences and gates. Don't trespass—ask permission before entering private property.

Photographs—published in magazines or books or actual prints and slides—are often the only resource we have, especially for older buildings that no longer exist, **11**. When trying to find photos of a particular building or area, try local historical societies or chambers of commerce. The Internet has become a terrific source—try keywords for the town and business name or type. I've purchased many real-photo postcards from eBay and other sources and found images that others have posted online. If you're lucky, you may find multiple photos to work with; in many cases, we have to try to build a model from a single image.

You don't need to make detailed scale drawings to scratchbuild a structure. However, at minimum you'll find it handy to sketch out walls with dimensions and mark door and window locations. You'll also need to determine how to approach corner joints, roof construction, and any other special features.

In trying to determine dimensions from photos, look for things with known sizes. Check doorways: if you can determine that an entry door is about 80" tall (a common size), it can

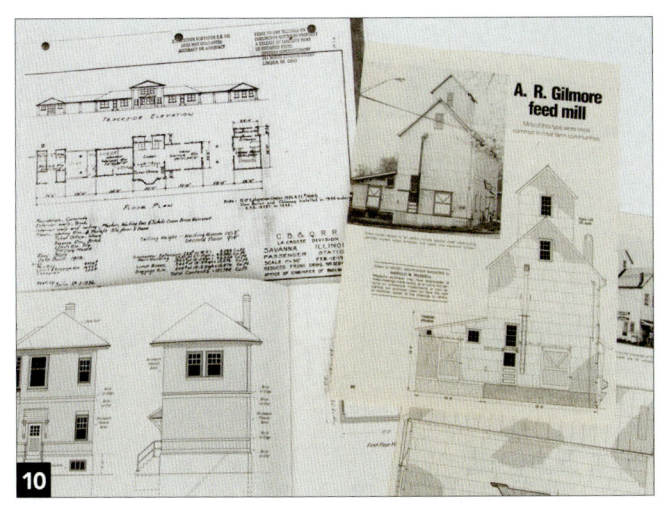

10 It's best to start with published plans if possible, such as those from a magazine (right) or book (lower left). The drawings at upper left (depot drawings from a railroad historical society) aren't highly detailed, but they provide a good starting point.

11 I had to guesstimate the dimensions of this Illinois Central interlocking tower at Portage, Ill., based on this photo and several others. I used a computer graphics program, but you can simply sketch it on paper.

12 I used a mechanical pencil to trace the wall dimensions on Evergreen clapboard sheet. A Micro-Mark right-angle cutter makes quick work of cutting out window openings.

13 A good way to do corners with simulated wood siding is to glue walls to a square corner post. This works with wood or plastic structures.

14 Beveling corners requires care. You can file them, as here, use a sanding block, or scrape the edge with a knife. Test-fit the corner before adding glue.

help you determine the overall wall dimensions. You can also count courses of bricks, blocks, or the number of boards in clapboard siding. Look for other objects as well. For example, a 40-foot boxcar can indicate structure size.

It can also help to resize a photo to match the modeling scale and print it out after straightening it (correcting any skew or proportional issues). (Chapter 8 has details on printing out scale-size photos of walls and complete structures).

For large structures, such as a railroad station and many industrial buildings, a structure built to full scale size would overwhelm a scene on even a large layout. Because of this, the technique of selective compression is popular among model railroaders.

Selective compression simply means building a structure that captures the appearance and flavor of the real thing, but making it smaller to make it better fit a scene on a layout.

You can compress a structure in several ways. You can eliminate a floor (make it three stories instead of four), reduce overall dimensions by 5 to 15 percent (while keeping doors to scale size), or simply shorten wall lengths (for example, providing a loading dock with room for four boxcars instead of seven).

Determine the materials you'll be using for the project. Make sure you have enough on hand for the structure—you don't want to come up a couple inches short on a wall or discover you need two more window frames at 10 p.m. on a Saturday night.

If you're using textured sheet material for the walls, decide if the sheet is heavy enough for the walls themselves (usually fine for styrene sheets). For thin material and large walls, you may want to apply the material over a core of plain styrene sheet.

Basic techniques

Once you have at least a good sketch with dimensions and a plan of the structure, you can begin construction. Walls are a good place to start. You can lay out the dimensions directly on the material, as I did with the interlocking tower. I used a mechanical pencil to trace the wall outlines and window openings on Evergreen clapboard styrene sheet.

I recommend cutting out windows

15 A tight fit between the walls results in an apparently seamless corner joint.

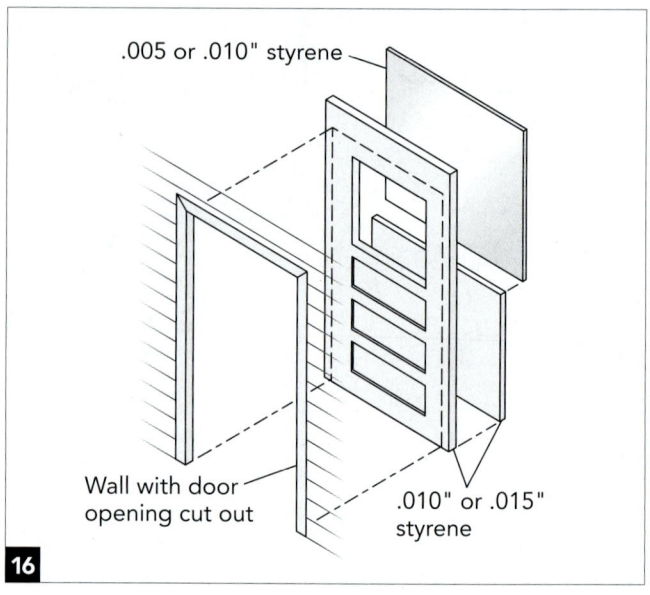

16 Panel doors are easy to make with multiple layers of thin sheet styrene.

before cutting walls apart. You can cut windows in sheet wood or styrene with a straightedge and hobby knife, holding the straightedge firmly and using multiple passes with the knife. This works well for thin material (under .040"), but can be tedious for thicker material or for structures having lots of windows.

An effective technique is to drill a hole in the center of the opening and use a chisel-tip knife to cut lines to each corner from the center. This makes it easier to scribe and snap the resulting four pieces from the opening.

One of my favorite tools for cutting windows is the corner cutter from Micro-Mark, which you can use two ways, **12**. You can use it like a punch, by positioning it in a window corner and tapping it with a hammer, or you can place it in a drill press (not turning) and pull down the press handle to cut the material.

Drilling a hole in the middle of each opening helps when using the punch, making it less likely to distort the material while you are cutting it. You may have to clean up the opening slightly with a file or hobby knife.

Corners can be handled several ways. With clapboard and other types of replicated wood siding, adjoining walls can be glued to square strips to simulate vertical corner trim pieces, **13**. The square strip should be slightly larger than the thickness of the wall material. Glue one wall to the strip on a flat surface. When that's dry, glue the corner together with any of the techniques described in chapter 2.

For brick, the best method is to bevel the mating edges, **14**. You want the joint to be as tight as possible, with mortar lines aligning, so the corner bricks look like single pieces, **15**. Depending upon the thickness of the material and the height of the walls, you can do this by using a hobby knife, a miter saw, a sander, or a large flat file. As you're creating the bevels, check the mating edges frequently to make sure you don't remove too much material.

With either of the above methods, gluing a length of square strip or another type of brace inside the corner joint adds strength.

Adding windows, doors, and roofs

Depending upon whether you are using commercial window and door frames or making your own, and whether the windows are a different color than the walls, you may want to add these items before or after assembling the walls into a shell. (As chapter 7 explains, painting structures in subassemblies is a good idea if possible.)

If you're using commercial plastic or metal castings, adding them is usually a simple matter of providing a proper-sized hole, painting the casting (if it's a different color than the wall), and gluing it in place (after painting the walls). You can also modify window castings by trimming away mullions or adding new ones with thin strip styrene.

It's relatively easy to make panel-style doors in almost any pattern, **16**. Simply cut out the panels from .010" styrene (.005" for N scale and .020" for O scale) and glue them to a piece of plain styrene.

I finished the interlocking tower by adding a four-piece roof cut from Pikestuff sheet shingle material (plastic), **17**. The chimney is made from four pieces of brick sheet cut to size and beveled.

You have other options besides textured sheet material. Rolled roofing can be applied in similar fashion to the wood depot in chapter 2. For flat roofs, you can paint sheet styrene grimy black, and then simulate roofing seams by painting darker black lines, **18**. You can also scribe seam lines into the plastic before painting.

Some flat roofs are covered with gravel. You can simulate this by painting the roof a shade of gray to dark gray or grimy black and sprinkling fine ballast over it, **19**. By adding the ballast while the paint is wet, the paint bonds it in place. Then press the ballast in place and let it dry, **20**.

17 The finished interlocking tower captures the appearance of the prototype. Nobody will know if the model's dimensions exactly match those of the real tower.

18 You can paint flat roofs grimy black and roofing seam lines black. Seams can also be scribed into the roof before painting.

19 To simulate a gravel-coated roof, paint the roof with a heavy coat of acrylic paint and then sprinkle fine ballast over the wet paint.

20 Press the ballast in place, let it dry, and tip the building to remove the excess. Add another coat if needed by brushing the first coat with matte medium and reapplying the ballast.

Complex structures

The more complex the structure is, the more detailed your drawings and plan should be. I wanted to build a model of a Swift & Co. packing company branch house. These were destinations for refrigerator cars from the company's packing plants, and were located across the country. Most had a similar appearance. The best photo I could find was a Library of Congress color image taken in 1941, **2**. I used this as my starting point, although I altered a few details.

In determining dimensions, I took some educated guesses based on the height of the people standing in front of the building and the size of the vehicles in the photo. Instead of sketching the walls, I imported the photo into Adobe Photoshop Elements, used the "skew" and "transform" tools to correct the perspective for both visible walls (see chapter 8 for more on that process), resized the images to HO scale, and printed them out. I glued the printouts to cardstock and taped the walls together, **21**. Adding a couple of vehicles and a refrigerator car to the scene helped me judge whether the overall size and dimensions were in the ballpark.

I used the cardboard mock-up to determine the dimensions of all of the various features on the building, simply writing all the dimensions on the mock-up itself, **22**. I double-checked the dimensions on every side to make sure everything added up correctly.

This building had a variety of features, including brick panels, concrete columns and horizontal pieces, and large windows. I toyed with a number of possible construction methods, and finally settled on using clear acrylic (Plexiglas) as a shell and layering other materials atop it.

Acrylic sheet is strong and has the advantage of being built-in window glazing. Styrene materials and components (sheet brick, styrene strip, window frames, and doors) can be glued directly to the acrylic surface with liquid plastic cement. To get a feel for the material, I played around a bit by gluing several items to it.

41

21 Sizing a photo, printing it out, gluing it to cardstock, and taping it together is a great way to test how a building will look in a finished scene.

22 I determined the dimensions of the windows and trim by measuring the mock-up. I wrote the dimensions and other notes directly on the photo prints.

23 To cut straight lines in acrylic, scribe it along the cut line with a utility knife, then bend it at the line (the edge of a table helps). It will snap cleanly at the line. Keep the protective covering on the acrylic as long as possible.

24 You can cut inside corners and curves in acrylic with a coping saw. Clamp the sheet to ensure a smooth cut. The 1x2 guides the saw for straight cuts.

I couldn't find any commercial window frames that captured the look of the real ones, and I wasn't looking forward to the prospect of building that many windows mullion-by-mullion with strip styrene. After some experimenting, I decided to scribe the mullions into the surface of the acrylic, and then use paint to fill the scribe lines. This technique is not perfect (especially if you look really closely), but it worked well enough to capture the overall appearance.

You can use these same basic techniques to make large structures or backdrop walls and flats in industrial areas, or to make high-rise buildings in cities.

Forming walls and windows

I bought two 12" x 48" cutoffs of Plexiglas .125" clear acrylic from the bargain bin of a local plastics wholesaler. I measured and cut the four walls, leaving the protective paper on the acrylic. (Make sure you know which walls are overlapping the others.)

Acrylic handles like thick styrene—the scribe-and-snap technique works well for cutting and leaves square edges. Use a utility knife to scribe the cut line a couple of times and then snap the material at the line, **23**.

As an alternative, you can cut acrylic sheet with a table saw or miter saw. The key is to mount the blade backward (this will keep edges from chipping) and feed the sheet at moderate speed. Don't force it, but don't go so slowly that it begins to melt.

For the two walls with notches, first mark the cut lines and then clamp the wall to a table. Use a coping saw to cut along each line, **24**. A wood block works well for a guide. Clean up the edges as needed with a file or sanding block.

Lay out the windows on each wall, marking the dimensions on the protective paper with a pencil. I used a combination square to keep everything aligned. Once you're sure everything is marked properly, use a hobby knife to

25 Cut the window openings in the protective paper with a hobby knife and then peel those areas away.

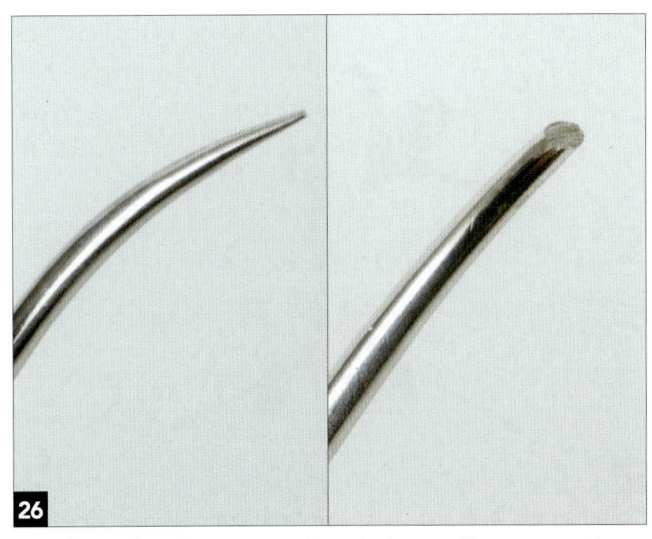

26 I used two dental picks to scribe window mullions: one with the original pointed tip (left), and another with a tip that I filed to a wider shape for wider mullions (right).

27 Use a square for keeping scribed lines aligned and make several passes with the scriber.

28 Scrape remnants away with a piece of wood cut to a chisel tip. The wood won't mar the acrylic surface.

29 Use a foam brush to spread artist's tube acrylic paint across the windows. The paint will settle in the scribed lines.

30 Lightly rub the surface with a thin cloth or paper towel to remove paint from the window area.

31 Clamping the walls to a 1x2 helps keep them aligned for gluing. Test-fit the joint before adding cement.

32 Acrylic cement will provide the strongest bond. Run a bead along the mating edge, then re-clamp the pieces.

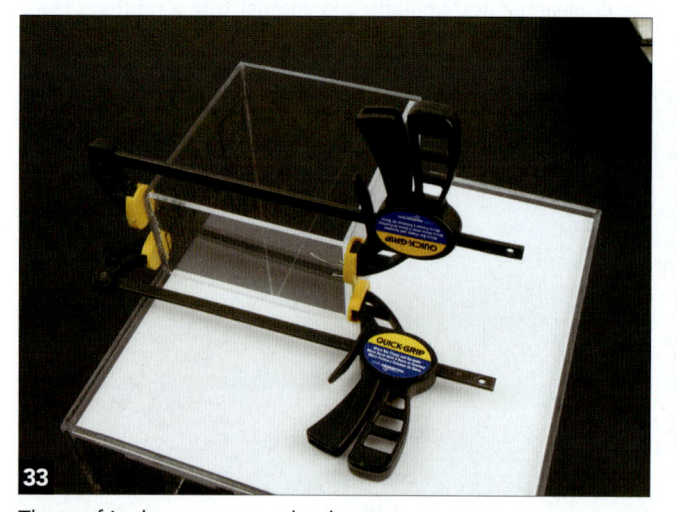

33 The roof is sheet styrene, glued to styrene strip supports cemented to the inside of the walls. Clamp and glue the fourth-story walls in place as with the other walls.

34 The completed building shell is now ready for the addition of detail overlays.

cut the window openings in the paper and peel off the window areas, **25**.

Now comes the time-consuming part: scribing the mullions. There are a lot of them—each window is a scale 12" wide and 18" tall. I used a pointed dental pick for the narrow mullions. To scribe the wider parts of the frame, I modified another dental pick by filing it to a flatter shape, **26**.

I marked the frame and mullion locations next to the windows with a pencil and used a small steel square as a scribing guide, **27**. Work slowly and carefully. I made three passes for each line, holding the square firmly so that it didn't slip. This process can be tedious—take some breaks, and don't try to do them all at once.

Once the lines are all scribed, clean the lines and shell surface of all remaining bits of acrylic. I cut a large piece of stripwood to a chisel tip and used it to scrape over the lines (the wood won't mar the surface), **28**. I then scrubbed the surface with a stiff bristle brush to get rid of any lingering acrylic flakes.

To color the window frames and mullions, I used artist's tube acrylic mars black paint. I dabbed it across the surface with a foam brush, using the flat surface of the foam to smear the paint diagonally across the scribed patterns, **29**. Once the paint dried, I rubbed the paint from the acrylic surface with a paper towel, **30**. Use light pressure—if you press too hard, you'll remove the paint from the grooves.

This method isn't perfect. You'll still be left with some paint flecks around the edges of the grooves, which you can remove with the stripwood chisel. You'll also have to use a fine-point brush to add black paint to any grooves where the paint didn't stick originally.

Construction

Begin gluing the walls together. I clamped two walls against a 1x2, making sure they were aligned, with the proper wall overlapping the other, **31**. I then removed the overlapping wall and ran a bead of acrylic cement (I used Weld-On SciGrip no. 16) on the end of the wall and re-clamped the other wall, **32**.

Something I learned after this joint: the glue oozed out a bit and stuck to the wood, making it tough to remove

35 Fit a corner L piece in place, mark its length, and cut it to fit. Glue it in place with gel liquid plastic cement applied to the rear.

36 Cutting all horizontal trim pieces with a NorthWest Chopper and using a stop ensures that all pieces will be the same length.

37 Glue the horizontal styrene and brick strips in place, starting at the bottom. Make sure they fit snugly against each other and that all parts are square.

38 Add the first vertical styrene strip, making sure it butts firmly against the horizontal pieces. Continue adding pieces along the wall.

Cutting styrene

You can cut very thin sheet styrene (.005" and .010") with a hobby knife. Press down lightly with the knife blade and use multiple passes.

Medium (.020" to .080") sheet styrene is easily cut with the scribe-and-snap technique. Scribe the cut line once or twice with a knife and then bend the styrene at the scribe. It will break cleanly, with minimal cleanup needed.

Thick styrene (.100" to .125" and thicker) sometimes won't break cleanly. When you need a very clean cut on thick styrene (or medium sheets over .060"), use a utility knife instead of a hobby knife. The blades are tougher, the tip won't break, and you'll need less effort and fewer passes.

The scribe-and-snap method also works for thin textured material, such as Evergreen and Plastruct sheets, but not as well with injection-molded wall sections. For these, I recommend using a utility knife or razor saw.

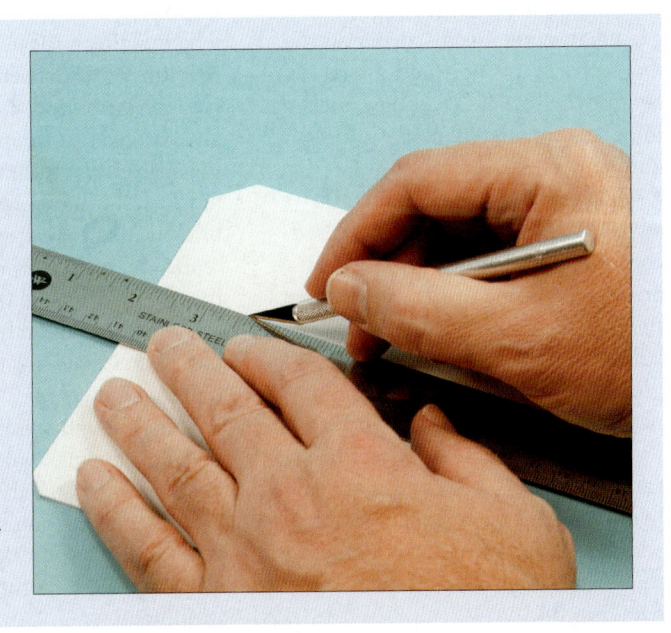

45

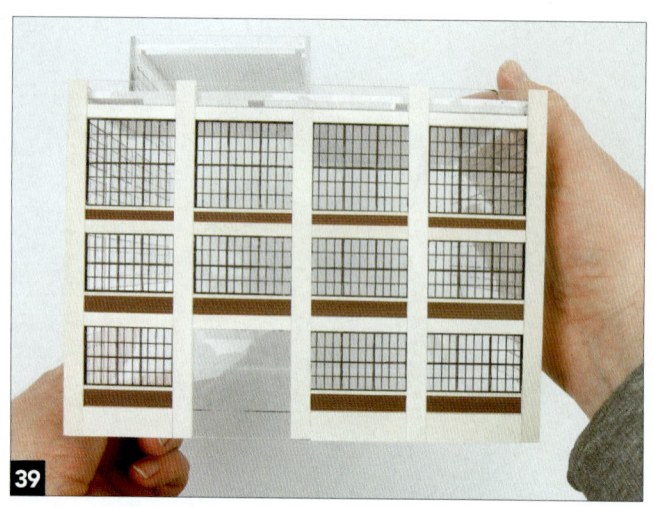

39 All panels on the front are now done, except for the door area and the top brick trim.

40 The entry door at right is from Pikestuff, and the large doors are made from scribed styrene with strip styrene trim.

41 The decorative trim pieces are .010" styrene sheet, cut to shape, painted concrete color, and glued directly to the brick.

42 Glue the wall caps in place with liquid plastic cement. Start at one corner and work your way around the building, making sure each joint is snug.

the walls. For the remaining joints, I carved away the inside corner on the 1x2 so there was no wood directly against the corner. Make sure each joint sets completely before adding another wall.

Add the roof. I used plain .100" styrene sheet, notched for the raised corner section. I glued styrene strips around the inside of the walls so that the roof would rest a scale foot or so below the tops of the walls. I then glued the roof in place with liquid plastic cement.

The inner fourth-story sections came next, **33**. Glue them in the same manner as the other walls, and then add a styrene roof in place. The basic shell is now finished and ready for detailing, **34**.

Building materials
The building surface is a mix of brick (Plastruct brick sheet) and concrete (styrene strips and sheet cut to size and painted). You can see the widths of the strips needed that I marked on the mock-up in photo **22**. The Plastruct brick is .022" thick, and the styrene "concrete" had to project farther than the brick, so I used .060" styrene for the wide horizontal base and vertical pieces, and .040" for the narrower horizontal pieces.

I cut enough styrene to size for the project, allowing some extra in case I miscut anything. I also glued the corner pieces together (one for each corner) in an L and test-fit them to make sure they aligned properly with the windows.

Paint all of the brick and styrene prior to adding them to the building. For the brick, I used a boxcar red color and then gave it a very light wash of gray mixed with the red (see chapter 6 for details). I did this to a few sheets of material and cut strips to the needed width. I airbrushed all of the styrene pieces with a light concrete mix—I used a Polly Scale mix of 10 parts white, 3 parts aged concrete, and 1 part undercoat light gray.

Start at a corner. Lay a piece of corner L trim in place, mark it, cut it with a razor saw, and glue it in place with liquid plastic cement, **35**. Measure the width of the first window area and cut a piece of the base styrene to length, setting the fence on a NorthWest Short Line Chopper to

43 Bend each arched roof cap before gluing it in place. Leave extra material on each end so you can trim it.

44 File the cap to shape. Masking tape protects the wall. Add the side trim, repeat the filing process, and touch up the area with paint.

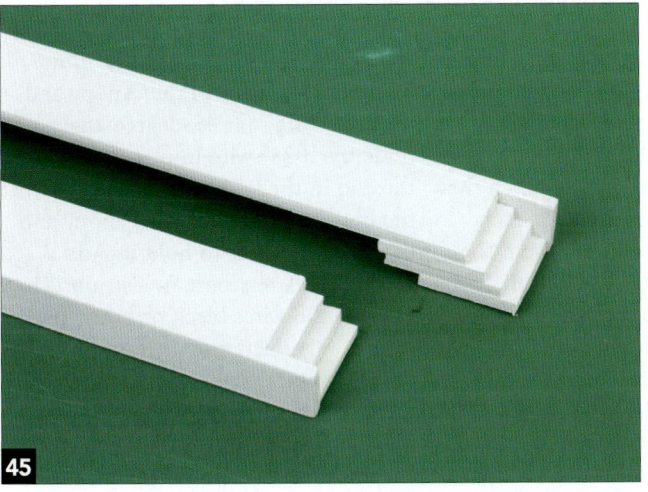

45 The concrete loading docks are made from layers of .100" styrene with a vertical facing strip.

46 The canopy is .040" styrene with an I beam for trim. Glue the mounting wires in holes in the pilasters, bend them under the canopy, and glue them in place. Note the C channel on the wall.

47 Add a drop of CA to the rear of each letter and then carefully place it with tweezers.

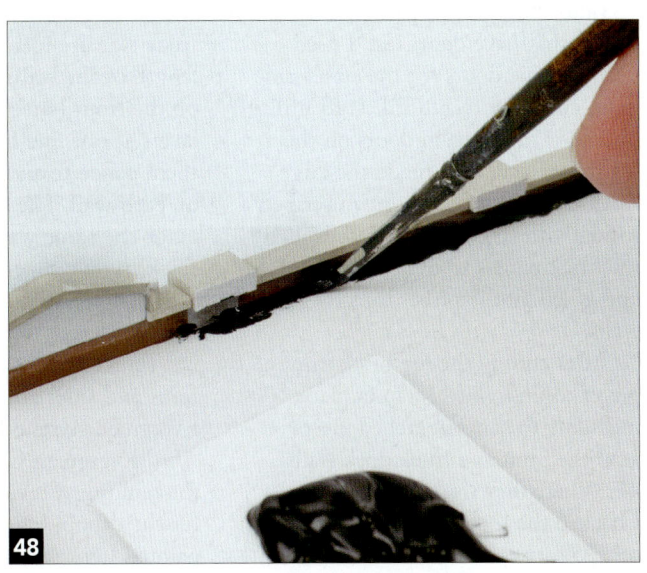

48 I sealed the edges of the roof with black artist's tube acrylic paint, which resembles roofing tar.

49 Roof details include vents, an air-conditioning unit, a roof access doorway, and a smokestack.

50 The rear wall has no windows, just large brick panels between the vertical and horizontal concrete strips.

ensure that all trim pieces for this section are exactly the same length, **36**.

Begin gluing the horizontal pieces in place, starting at the bottom, **37**. A drafting square placed against the corner piece can help things stay aligned. I used a dab of gel-type glue on the back of each piece, and then touched a brush of liquid plastic cement to an edge once it's in place.

Repeat the process until all horizontal pieces for a section are in place, and then add the next vertical piece, **38**. Repeat the process until the entire wall is done and proceed to the next wall, **39**. As photos of the finished building show, the rear has no windows—just large brick panels.

I did the top trim panels and the panels that have doors last. I used Grandt Line doors for the street-side main entry doors and Pikestuff utility doors for the walk-in doors on the loading docks, **40**. I made the large freight doors from Evergreen scribed siding with strip styrene frames. I cut the brick panels to fit around the doors and glued all the pieces directly to the walls.

After cutting the top brick trim pieces to fit, I glued them in place, including the angled/arched pieces atop the front and truck dock walls, **41**. Where they rise above wall level, I backed the tops of these with scraps of .125" styrene to match the wall thickness. The decorative pieces are .010" sheet styrene, eyeballed to match the basic shape of the prototype pieces, and painted with the light concrete mix.

Then I added the wall caps, **42**. These are .060" x .100" strips, with pieces of .125" styrene cut to match the width of the vertical pilasters at each pilaster and corner. I painted them the concrete trim color. The caps over the arched pieces look tricky, but they're not. Scribe a mark on the underside at the bend point. You can then bend it roughly to shape and glue it in place, **43**. Leave extra material at each end and then file it to shape when the glue is dry, **44**. Add the vertical piece, file it to match, and touch up the paint.

The loading docks are made from .100" styrene, cut to a scale 6-foot width. The docks on the rail side and truck side are identical, spanning the length of the wall, but both have steps on the front (street) side, **45**. Gluing layers at one end forms steps. Paint them concrete and glue them in place on each wall. The street-side steps are made the same way, by simply layering thick styrene sheet.

The loading dock canopies are .040" styrene, a scale 6 feet wide and just shorter than the wall length. The front and sides are trimmed with .080" Evergreen styrene I beam. A length of .100" Evergreen C channel, glued to the building, provides a mounting base for the canopy, **46**. The canopies are painted light gray.

The canopies are further strengthened by five 45-degree support wires (one at each pilaster). Drill no. 69 mounting holes in the canopy and in the building (at 45-degree angles). Slide the .028" wire in place and glue the end in the building with CA. Trim the bottom end below the canopy and bend the end over to hold it. Add a touch of CA to secure it. Use a brush to paint the wires black or grimy black.

The raised lettering is from Slater's 6mm styrene alphabet set. I painted the letters with gold craft paint prior to adding them. Test the spacing (see chapter 7) before applying them for good. Add a bit of CA to the rear of the first letter and carefully set it in place, **47**. Repeat the process for each letter.

For the roof, I brushed artist's black acrylic tube paint along the seam between the edge of the roof and walls, **48**. I kept this thick to represent roofing/sealing tar. The roof itself is painted grimy black. Roof details include an air-conditioning unit and large vents from a Walthers detail set, two smaller vents from a City Classics roof detail set, and an access door/housing and smokestack from my scrapbox, **49**.

I added a piece of white mat board behind the front wall upper windows to match the appearance of the prototype photo. I also added an interior view block of black construction paper to keep people from looking all the way through the building (see chapter 5 for details). You can see the rear of the building in photo **50**.

1

CHAPTER FIVE

Interior detailing and lighting

Few structure kits include interior details. However, with the large windows found on many structures, the lack of details makes otherwise nice buildings look abandoned and lifeless. Adding even a few basic interior details makes a structure look like it serves an actual purpose, **1**.

Interior details—figures and appliances in the appliance store, shelving in the market at right, and signs in both structures' windows—make buildings look like they serve a definite purpose and help give life to scenes.

49

2 A black construction paper view block keeps people from looking in one window and out another. This is the Swift branch house from chapter 4.

3 City Classics makes several sets of HO scale curtains and window blinds. The acetate pieces can be cut and glued inside window openings.

4 Thin cardstock or paper can be glued behind windows at varying heights to represent blinds and shades.

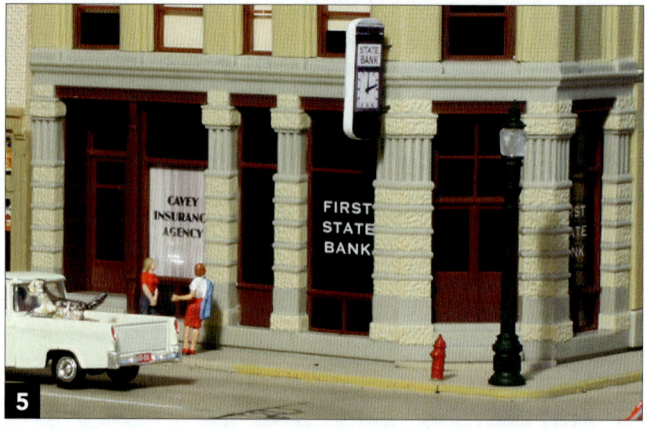

5 The Cavey Insurance and bank signs were designed on a computer, printed on paper, and glued directly behind the clear styrene window glazing. They nicely hide the lack of interior detail in this HO Walthers building.

You can take interior detailing to various levels, from adding a few simple window treatments and signs to a complete interior with furniture and figures. First, consider a structure's placement and its visibility on your layout. Buildings near the layout edge, those having large windows, or ones in areas where you plan to do a lot of photography, needs more interior detailing than do structures that reside in the background.

Window treatments

At a minimum, most structures require some type of view block to keep people from looking in a window and seeing out another one, which makes a lack of interior detail obvious. This is especially true if you can see into a window on one floor and out a window on a different floor.

Thin black cardboard or construction paper works well as a view block, **2**. You can simply cut a piece of cardboard that fits from corner to corner or one that loops from one front corner to the other, depending upon the angle at which the structure is viewed. Larger structures may require more complex view blocks, but that's just a matter of adding another piece of paper or two.

Simple window coverings add visual interest, and they're often sufficient for hiding the interiors on background models. Most windows on real buildings have some type of interior covering, such as blinds, pull-down shades, or curtains. City Classics makes an HO line of window coverings with various styles of curtains and shades, **3**. Printed on clear acetate, they can be glued in place as window glazing or glued behind the model's existing clear glazing.

Pull-down shades can be simulated in any scale by simply gluing cardstock or paper behind window glazing, **4**. These shades are often off-white but can be found in other colors. (I often use old manila file folders.) For more visual interest, vary their heights and make some shades (and windows) partially open and some fully covered.

You can also make your own window coverings by taking photos and using the prints or by manipulating the images with photo-editing software and then printing them. Photo-editing software allows you to combine window coverings or a black background with letters to make it look like the window has painted-on lettering, **5**. Many commercial buildings, such as shops and stores,

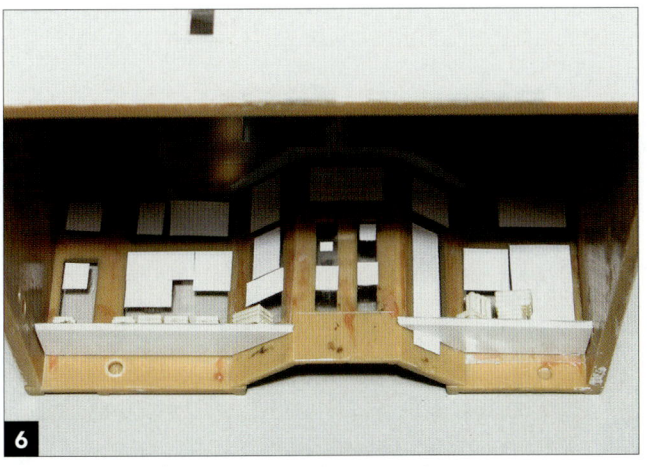

6 Adding a few details in the windows—such as some Preiser crates and signs in this HO DPM storefront building—gives the impression of an interior.

7 Under normal viewing conditions, it's difficult to see more than a few scale feet into a building

8 Spray a coat of clear flat finish onto clear styrene to create a frosted or glazed glass appearance. This is an HO grain elevator from Walthers.

9 This HO laser-cut depot kit included scribed wood interior flooring. It serves as a base for interior details including crates, desks, chairs, and figures.

have paper signs placed in the windows (see chapter 7).

For many model structures without interior lighting, it's difficult to see more than a few scale feet into the windows. Along with window coverings, a few basic details placed directly behind the window are often enough to convey the impression of an interior, **6**. For example, in a retail store, a few window signs and some crates or a small window display are more than sufficient, **7**.

Frosted window glazing can also effectively hide the lack of an interior. Simply spray clear styrene with a light coat of flat finish. This effectively captures the look of grimy factory windows or frosted glass, **8**. The glazing can be installed either dull-side out or dull-side in to vary the appearance.

Preparation and details

For more extensive detailing, it's good to have a plan for each structure. Determine how much detail you need by a structure's placement on your layout and the size of its windows. You'll also need more detail if you plan to light a structure's interior.

In the area to be detailed, you'll need to have a solid floor. If a kit includes an interior floor, you can usually use it, **9**; otherwise, cut a piece of styrene to fit and glue it in place. You can limit the area to be detailed by adding a rear wall or side walls to the floor. You can also build small shadowboxes that can be added to structures (more on those in a bit).

Mat board makes good interior walls and floors, and it is much easier than painting other materials.

It's available in a wide variety of colors, as well as some patterns, **10**. Local frame shops usually sell inexpensive packages of scrap pieces, which are large enough for interior walls.

A number of commercial products are available that you can use for interior details, with the widest selection in HO, **11**. You can find tables, chairs, desks, other furniture, machinery, crates, boxes, tools, stoves, soda machines, and many other items. Detail sets are also made specifically for businesses such as gas stations, offices, and retail stores. Check the Walthers catalog and websites of companies such as Bar Mills, Busch, Durango Press, Evergreen Hill Designs, Heki, JL Innovative Design, Preiser, Scale Structures Ltd., and Sequoia Scale Models.

10 Mat board works well for interior walls. It comes in a wide variety of colors and is easy to cut and glue.

11 Many details are available, including HO chairs and figures from Preiser and desks and cabinets from Heki.

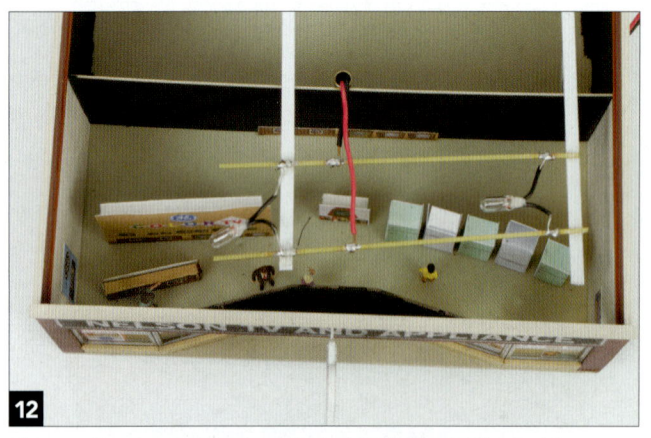

12 This appliance store interior includes "Color TV" graphics (made with Adobe Photoshop). The televisions and refrigerators started as photographs, were printed on photo paper, and then cut and glued together.

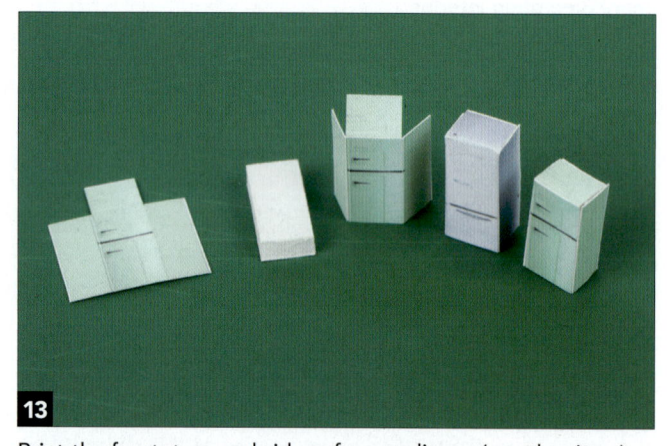

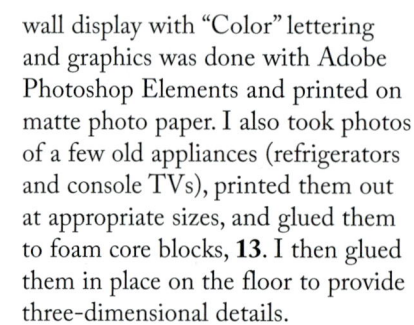

13 Print the front, top, and sides of an appliance (or other item) together. Lightly scribe the fold lines and glue it to a foam core or wood block.

Depending upon the manufacturer, these details are available as unpainted metal, unpainted resin castings, or injection-molded styrene in various colors. Most of the time, details will require painting. And don't forget figures: Preiser, Woodland Scenics, and others make a tremendous variety of people that can be placed inside structures.

As with signs, you can make a variety of interior details with your computer, starting with some photos and various graphics. Using graphics software, you can create entire interior walls, shelving, and floors, as well as three-dimensional objects. Chapters 7 and 8 provide more details on how to manipulate and print images for doing this.

A few examples are shown in the appliance store in photo **12**. The back wall display with "Color" lettering and graphics was done with Adobe Photoshop Elements and printed on matte photo paper. I also took photos of a few old appliances (refrigerators and console TVs), printed them out at appropriate sizes, and glued them to foam core blocks, **13**. I then glued them in place on the floor to provide three-dimensional details.

To create 3-D objects, it helps if you can print the front, sides, and top together. You can then cut the piece out, lightly scribe the fold lines with a hobby knife, and fold the sides and top before gluing it to a block.

Another example is the HO City Classics grocery store in photo **14**. The windows are fairly large, showing the interior. I took photos of store shelving, blended them together (copy-pasting) in long strips, and printed them out.

They don't have to be highly detailed or positioned in precise rows like a store—they just need to be placed so that anyone looking through a window sees store shelves. I placed one strip in an arc around the rear walls, and two strips just inside the main windows, **15**.

Another great use of computer-manipulated graphics is making shipping cartons and stacks of cases. By taking photos of the sides, ends, and top of a cardboard case, for example, you can combine the views to make a stack of cartons as large as needed. I did this with several types of cartons (Campbell's Soup, Krispy Crackers, and Del Monte canned fruit), **16**.

I added these cases to the interior of the grocery wholesaler, including a combination of stacks on the floor, stacks on pallets, and flats glued to interior walls, **17**.

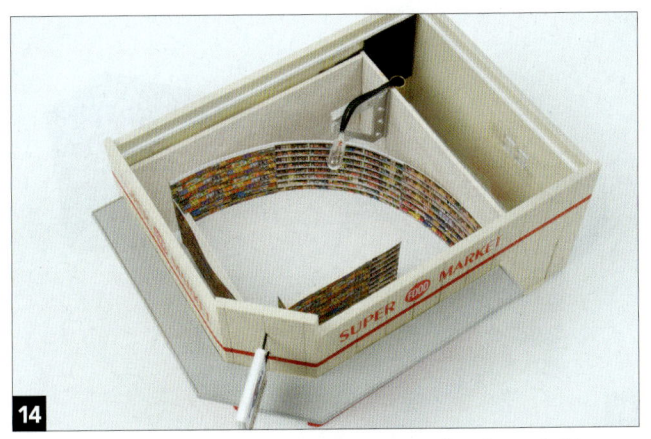

14 Photos of store shelves provide the interior for this HO City Classics store. A single Miniatronics bulb, run through a brass tube and mounted to a City Classics L-bracket, provides lighting.

15 The interior shelving is visible, but great detail is not needed. Window signs and an interior figure add additional detail.

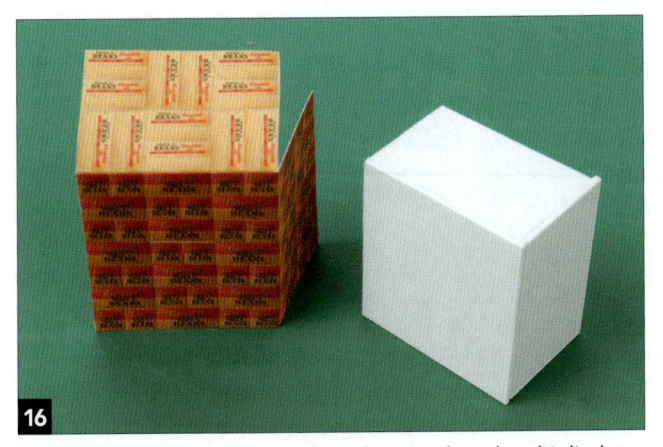

16 Photos of cartons can be combined, resized, and multiplied to create stacks of cases as large as needed. This one will be glued to a block made from thin sheet styrene at right.

17 Stacks of food cartons behind the open dock doors reinforce that this business is indeed a grocery wholesaler. This is the warehouse building from chapter 3.

Shadowboxes

A good option for many structures is to build small scenes in enclosed boxes and then glue the boxes in place behind windows and doors. These shadowboxes provide a great deal of detail in a small space, and can also be extended to fairly large areas. The warehouse building has several of them, including a small corner office and an area along the loading dock behind two large doorways, **18** and **19**.

You can build shadowboxes out of styrene sheet (.040" to .080"). Start by measuring the space needed and then assemble a floor and walls from styrene to fit the space. Use mat board for inner walls and glue the walls in place with small drops of cyanoacrylate adhesive (CA or super glue). You can also print your own walls if you want to simulate wallpaper or patterns.

Detail the walls with doors, bookcases, clocks, advertising signs, and other graphics (all easy to print on your own). Glue printouts in place with white glue. Follow this by adding details as needed: boxes, crates, furniture, figures, etc. Test-fit the shadowbox to make sure the details are in places where they can be seen.

You can see a shadowbox for an HO City Classics salon that I detailed as a barber shop in photo **20**. The box slides into place on the first floor of the structure and is glued in place with liquid plastic cement, **21**.

Remember that this detailing doesn't have to be perfect—you want to give the impression of a high level of detail, but viewers looking through windows and doorways won't be able to see small imperfections, and they won't be able to see the rear side of most interior details.

Interior lighting

If you operate your layout at night, interior structure lighting can add a great deal of atmosphere to the experience. You don't need to light every structure, but having select buildings (and rooms within buildings) illuminated, along with streetlights and other lighted details, helps create a distinctive mood, **22**.

You should decide whether to illuminate a structure early in the construction process. With some buildings, by the time you glue the roof and/or floor in place, it becomes very difficult to go back and add lighting.

Start by determining the type of lighting you want to install, and the specific areas of a structure that you want to illuminate. Some assembled buildings include an interior lamp, **23**. Unfortunately most of these have no interior, and a lighted building with no

53

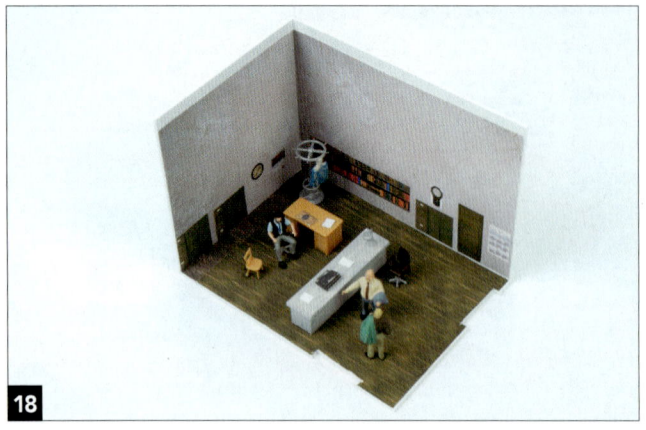

18 The warehouse office has printouts for walls, bookcases, filing cabinets, a clock, a door, and a wood floor, with desks, chairs, figures, and details from Preiser and others.

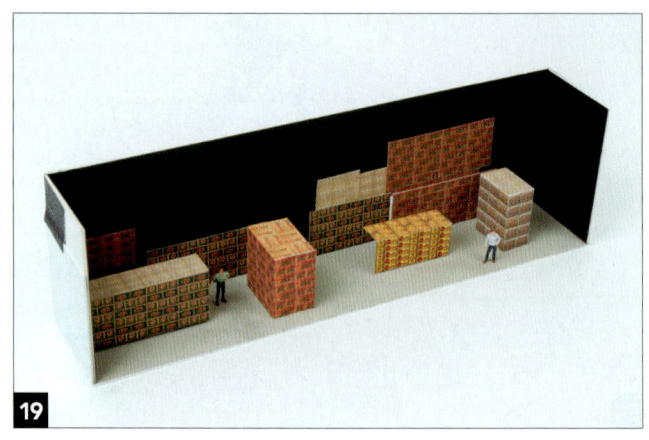

19 The loading dock shadowbox spans the two open loading-dock doors, with a figure visible in each door opening.

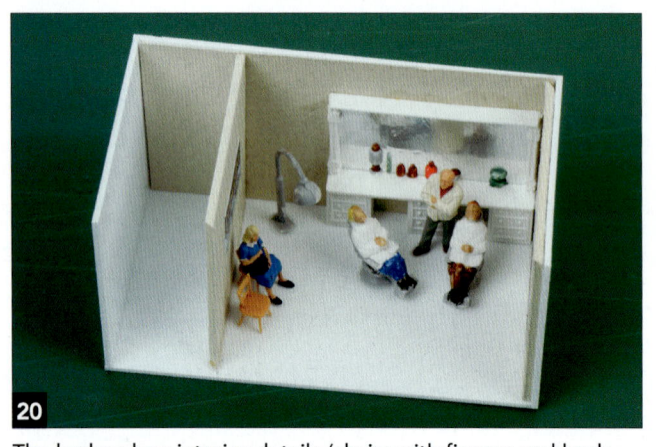

20 The barbershop interior details (chairs with figures and back counter) are from a Heki set. The box (styrene with mat board interior walls) is sized to fit into a City Classics building.

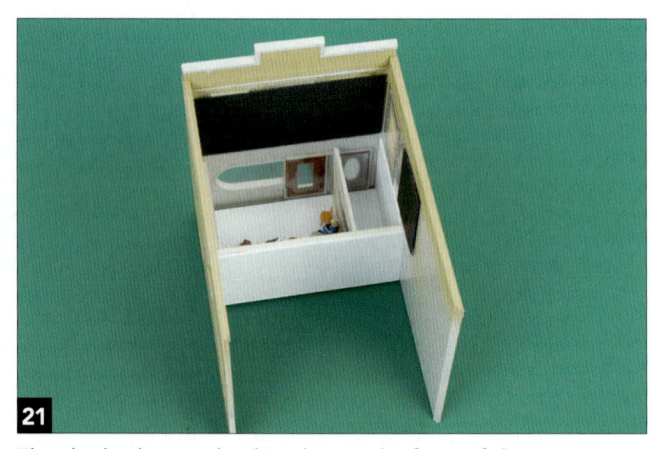

21 The shadowbox is glued in place in the front of the structure. The upper windows have blinds, but are covered with black construction paper as the building will be illuminated.

interior looks very stark and toylike, so you'll have to add some details, **24**.

Miniature light bulbs and light-emitting diodes (LEDs) are available from Bachmann, Brawa, Busch, Circuitron, Cir-Kit Concepts, Evan Designs, Faller, GRS Micro-Liting, Miniatronics, Model Power, Ngineering, Ram Track, Scale Shops, SoundTraxx, Walthers, Woodland Scenics, and other electronics suppliers.

Bulbs are the first choice for many modelers. They are available in a number of styles. Bachmann, Walthers (Life-Like), and others make bulbs that screw into bases that can easily be mounted on the underside of structure roofs, **25**.

Most miniature bulbs come with wire leads. These are typically sized in millimeters, with 5mm, 3mm (often called miniature or grain-of-wheat) common, down to 1mm and .75mm (called microminiature or grain-of-rice bulbs), **26**. Strings of clear holiday lights are another option. These can be cut from the string, providing their own bases and wiring leads.

Regardless of the size or style, you need to know each bulb's operating voltage. Bulbs are made in many voltage ratings, with the most common being 1.5V, 3V, 12V, 14V, and 18V. Holiday lights are typically 2.5V bulbs. Be sure to match the bulb voltage to your power supply. Bulbs will burn out if the voltage applied is above their rating, but they will last a long time if you power them just under their rating (for example, 12V for a 14V bulb). Larger, higher voltage bulbs are generally rated for much longer lives than small 1.5V bulbs, so I generally choose larger bulbs when possible.

Light-emitting diodes are another popular option for lighting, **27**. LEDs are more energy efficient, require less current than bulbs, and are available in bright white and a variety of other colors, but LED lighting is more directional in nature. LEDs also require current-limiting resistors to keep from burning out (see "LED resistor values" on page 56 for details).

It's a good idea to have a dedicated power supply for your layout lighting (interior lights, streetlights, etc.). This can be a regulated power supply or a plug-in transformer, which are available in a variety of voltage and amperage ratings (aee "Lighting circuits" on page 58 for more information).

Another option for interior lighting is the Just Plug lighting system, recently released by Woodland Scenics. This modular system includes LEDs in various colors, plug-in connectors,

22 Interior lighting, along with interior details, helps set a mood for evening operation. Lighting also helps viewers see interiors better during normal layout lighting conditions.

23 Some preassembled structures, like this Walthers HO storefront building, include an interior lamp.

24 You'll need to add interior details to avoid a stark, toylike appearance.

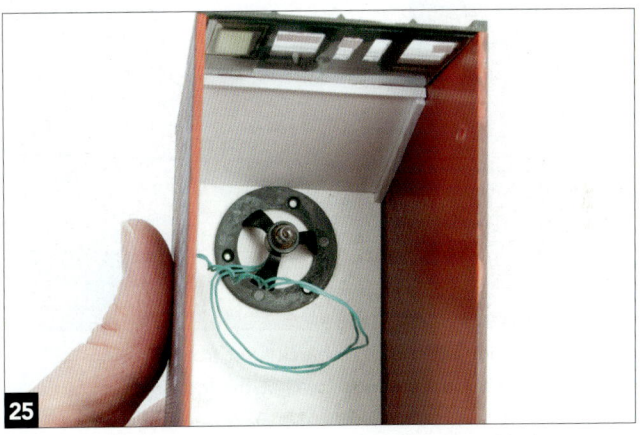

25 Walthers makes a bulb with a base that can be added to many structures. Here, it's installed in the Smalltown storefront building detailed as Webster's shoe store (photo 22).

switches, and power supplies, making it easy to add lighting effects without having to solder connections.

Preparing structures

The first step is to make sure there are no light leaks in a structure. This usually isn't a problem with wood buildings, but light will often glow through plastic structures, especially unpainted ones. Test structures and structure walls by shining a light on them from behind to see if any light shows through, **28**. If the surface glows, the interior wall must be covered (as with a mat board wall) or it should be painted black, **29**. (Don't forget the roof interior—a glowing roof isn't very realistic). It's a good idea to do this before adding any interior walls or detail, as it's very difficult to do this to a building that's already been detailed.

At the same time, test to make sure corners and other joints are tightly sealed, as light will find its way through any cracks. If light is showing through, run a bead of CA behind the corner and then paint it black.

By using the shadowbox interior detailing techniques, you lower chances of light leaks by illuminating only specific areas of a structure. However, you may need to add additional view blocks or interior walls to keep the light where you want it.

Decide how you want to light the structure. As you plan for bulb placement, double-check to make sure that the bulbs themselves won't be visible to viewers. Make sure they're located high enough above windows and doorways.

It's also a good idea to provide access to the bulbs for replacement and adjustment, either by making the roof removable or allowing access through the floor.

Adding lights

A small structure or small shadowbox often requires just a single bulb. I used a single ceiling-mounted fixture to light the HO shoe store (a Smalltown building) in photo **25**. The building has an interior shadowbox in the front half of the main floor, **30**. I added black mat board just behind the second-floor windows at front to both block the light and keep people from seeing inside. I also added City Classics window curtains and shades in all the top-floor windows.

The light fixture is a Life-Like structure lamp with base (no. 433-1205), which I simply glued in place with liquid plastic cement toward the front of the building above the interior. The roof is glued in place on this structure, which is OK because the

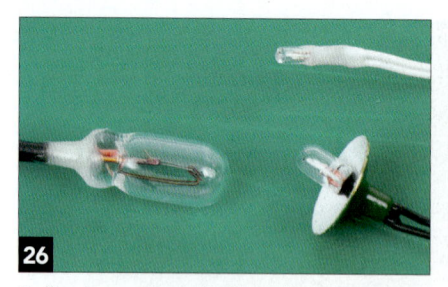

26 Bulbs come in many sizes, from this 5mm 12V miniature to a 1.5V microminiature (both from Miniatronics). Bulbs are also available with shades (also Miniatronics).

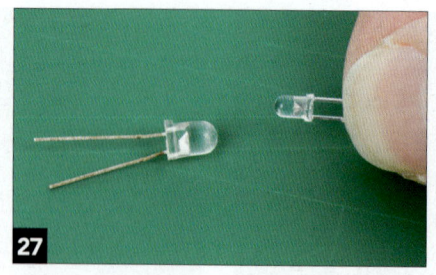

27 Light-emitting diodes (LEDs) are more directional in nature than bulbs but are more energy efficient. These are bright-white LEDs in 5mm and 3mm sizes.

28 Shine a light behind a wall to see if it glows through. If it does, the interior wall should be covered or painted.

29 Paint the interior wall black to block light from glowing through. This is the warehouse wall at the loading dock area.

30 The shoe store interior is a simple shadowbox with printed photos of shelving and several figures.

bulb in this fixture can be unscrewed and replaced from the bottom, as the building has an open area with no floor behind the shadowbox. This type of light works well in two-story and taller buildings where you can position the light above the scene being illuminated.

You can run wires from building lights directly through the scenery base to a lighting bus (main supply wires) under the layout, but I like to wire interior lights to connectors so it is easier to remove lights (and entire buildings) if needed, **31**. Miniatronics and others sell one- and two-wire micro connectors. Simply solder one end of the connectors to the wires from the light, and the other end to wires running to the lighting bus. You can then plug the light in place, **32**.

The supermarket in **14** and **15** shows a different approach. There wasn't enough ceiling headroom to add a fixture with a base, so I used a single standard 14V, 5.5mm bulb (Miniatronics no. 18-028-10), which provides plenty of light for the relatively small interior. I glued a piece of brass tube to the back of the rear interior wall, with a City Classics L brace in front of it (but behind the shelving graphics). The wires are simply glued in place with CA. When doing this, make sure that the bulb is not low enough to be visible when lit or tall enough that it contacts the roof.

I used another method with the appliance store in photo **33**. The interior is much larger, and the big display windows warranted more interior detailing. I decided to use two bulbs (the same 14V version as the

LED resistor values

Light-emitting diodes (LEDs) offer many possibilities in lighting, but they can't simply be plugged into your power bus. LEDs will burn out (quickly and dramatically) unless each is wired in series with a current-limiting resistor. The value of this resistor varies depending upon the input voltage.

White LEDs operate at a voltage around 3.2 to 3.5 volts, so they need a power supply of at least that voltage. For a 5V or 6V power supply, use a 120Ω resistor; for 9V, a 270Ω; and for 12V, 470Ω; for 14V to 18V, 1KΩ. It's a good idea to test an LED/resistor combination on your power bus before installing it in a structure. You can always try a larger resistor value; as long as the LED illuminates at a satisfactory level, it will be fine.

LEDs are DC devices. The anode requires the positive connection (generally indicated by having the longer lead) and the cathode the negative connection (the short lead; often with a flat spot on the side of the LED base).

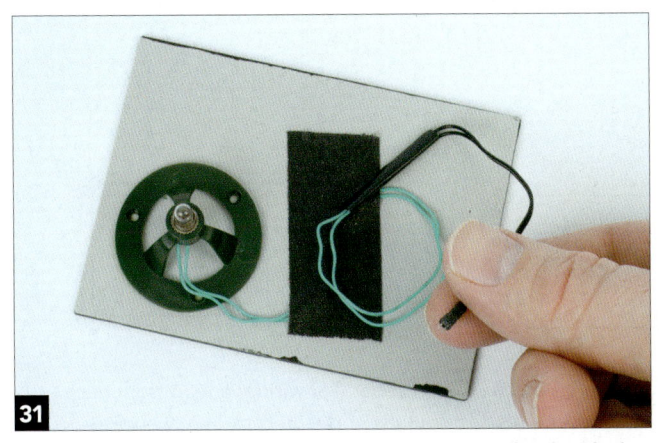

31 A two-pin connector is soldered to the lamp wire leads. Black gaffer tape holds the wires in place. Use electrical tape or shrink tubing to cover soldered joints.

32 Once the structure is being placed on the layout, simply plug the connectors together to power the light.

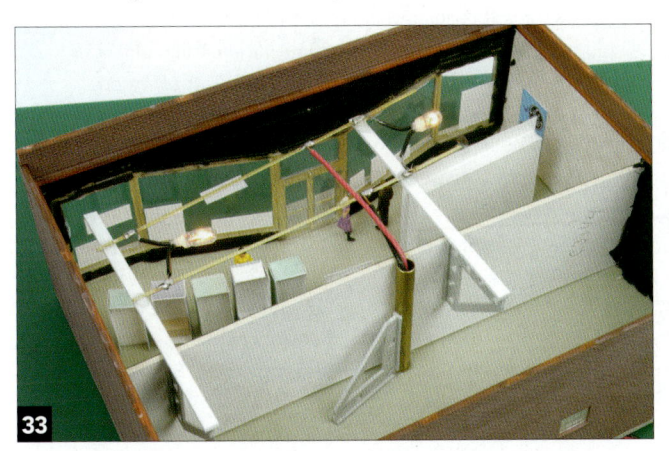

33 A pair of brass strips serves as the wiring bus in this HO structure. The leads for the two bulbs are soldered in place along the brass strips.

34 The two bulbs do a good job of evenly lighting the interior of the appliance store.

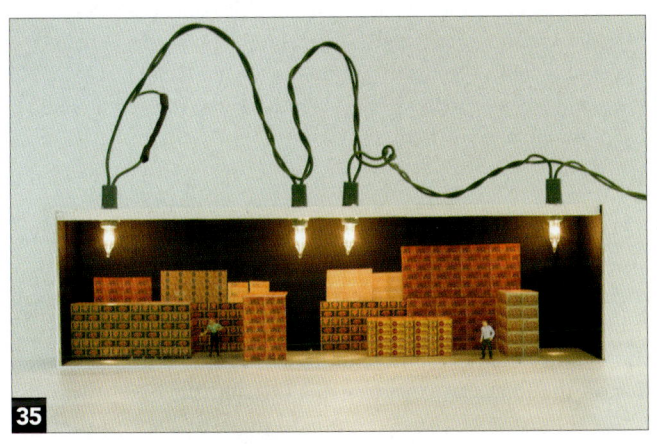

35 The holiday light mounting bases are simply pressed in place through holes in the foam-core ceiling. The lamps are spaced around the loading dock doors.

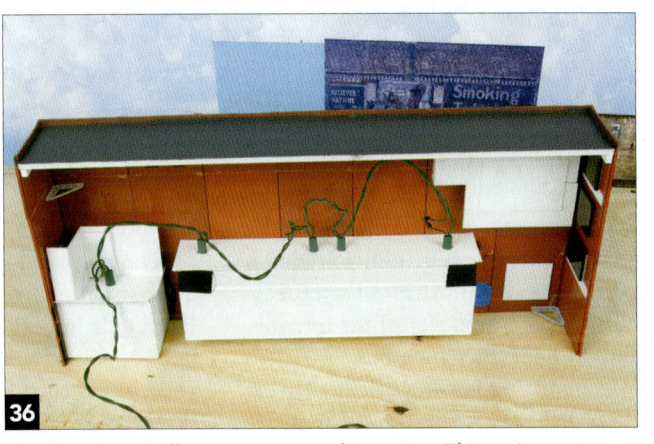

36 The five 2.5V bulbs are connected in series. This string can then be connected to the layout's 12V lighting bus.

supermarket) on an interior lighting bus to light the space. You can follow this technique for larger spaces by adding more bulbs and extending the bus.

This structure needed a removable roof since the interior requires a solid floor. The roof simply sets in place on the molded guides that run along the top of each wall. I had to modify the chimney at the rear, which was originally designed to be glued in place using an extension on the rear wall. I cut that extension off and glued a new chimney (from a City Classics roof detail kit) to the roof itself.

I drilled a hole in the floor just behind the rear interior wall and added

Lighting circuits

Series wiring

Parallel wiring

A regulated power supply, such as this one from Ngineering, is a much better option than an old power pack for powering structure lighting circuits.

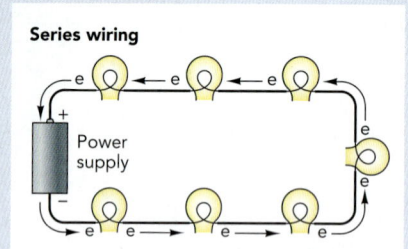

With series wiring, the leads of bulbs are daisy-chained to each other. This divides the bus/power supply voltage equally among all bulbs.

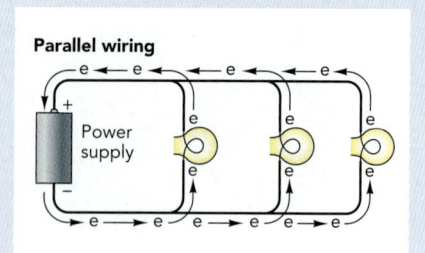

With parallel wiring, a lead from each bulb is connected to one bus wire. Each bulb receives the full voltage of the power supply.

Because bulbs come in so many voltage ratings, it's important to supply them with the proper voltage. Most larger bulbs (and most commercial accessories such as streetlights) are rated from 12V to 18V, with many microbulbs rated at 1.5V or 3V. I suggest either standardizing at one voltage or having two separate supplies.

I recommend installing a lighting bus (two wires supplying power for lights) around your layout. Use 16-gauge or 14-gauge wire to make sure that the bus can handle your power needs, and keep this bus separate from other wiring. You can then drop wires from each lighted accessory and structure to the lighting bus.

Use a dedicated power supply such as a plug-in wall transformer or regulated power supply. Bulbs can use AC or DC (LEDs require DC). Old power packs seem handy, but the voltage is often not regulated—meaning the actual output voltage can fluctuate depending upon the load. Likewise, using the variable DC output on an old power pack (which normally goes to the track) to supply a lower voltage is also risky, as if the speed control is accidentally dialed up, you risk blowing out your lights and LEDs.

The Ngineering no. N3512 shown is a 12-volt regulated DC plug-in transformer that supplies 1.25 amps. Similar power supplies are available from many suppliers in a variety of output voltage and amperage ratings.

You also need to figure out the current (amperage) draw for your lighting. Most larger (5mm) bulbs draw around 60 to 80 milliamps (mA; a milliamp is .001 amp), while many small 1.5V bulbs draw around 15 to 30 mA (the draw is often listed on the package). LEDs typically draw 15 to 20 mA. Add the ratings for all of the lamps on a circuit, and the total should be less than the rating of your supply.

For example: If you have 15 14V bulbs each rated at 80mA, figure 15 x .080 = 1.2A. A 12V supply rated at 1.25A will just cover it (powering 14V bulbs at 12V will extend bulb life and use less power); a 1.5A supply will give you a bit of leeway for expansion.

Bulbs can be wired in parallel or series as the drawings show. Parallel wiring provides the bus wiring's full voltage to each bulb. A bulb burning out doesn't affect other bulbs connected to the bus. Wiring bulbs in series divides the bus voltage among the bulbs. If one bulb burns out, the other bulbs wired in series will also go out.

a ¼" brass tube to hold the wiring. I then used L brackets (City Classics corner braces with strips of styrene atop them) to the rear of the interior wall to hold the wiring bus.

The wiring bus is a pair of .015" x .042" flat brass strips (Detail Associates no. 2528); you can also use brass rod or scrap pieces of brass or nickel silver rail. Cut them to run the length of the space you need to illuminate and use CA to secure them to the brackets. The bulb leads can then be soldered to the brass strips (two bulbs for this structure). Again, make sure that the bulbs aren't in contact with the roof when it is in place, **34**.

I used another approach with the warehouse building shown on page 26. That structure had two areas requiring lighting: a long shadowbox with two door openings along the freight dock, and a small corner office on the first floor.

I decided to use bulbs from a string of clear Christmas tree lights, with four of them over the warehouse area and one over the office. Each bulb is 2.5V, so by wiring them in series (a total rating of 5 x 2.5V = 12.5V), they can then be connected to the 12V lighting supply bus. They can also be controlled with a single on-off switch.

When using holiday lights, the first step is to cut off and discard the 110V house-current plug. The easiest way to use these bulbs is to use their mounting bases, which are conveniently wired. These bases can be glued to brackets inside structures, but the easiest way to use them is to press-fit the bases into foam core.

For the warehouse, I cut foam core ceilings to a press-fit over each shadowbox. I then used a hobby knife to cut a hole slightly smaller than the bulb mounting base in the foam core and pressed the bulb and base in place, **35**. Solder any connections needed before the bulbs are in place, **36**.

CHAPTER SIX

Painting and weathering

Once you have the ideal structure built, you're still not finished with it. Almost any model structure benefits from a good paint job. Wood kits require it, but most plastic kits and ready-built models—even those labeled "molded in realistic colors"—can be significantly improved and made more realistic with a coat or two of paint, **1**.

A good paint job and signs are vital to turning buildings into realistic, unique structures. These three plastic HO kits, from Smalltown USA, City Classics, and Walthers, can be found on thousands of other model railroads, but I would be willing to bet they are the only ones decorated as Webster's Shoes, Wally's Barber Shop, and Nelson TV and Appliance.

Acrylic model paints include Badger Modelflex, Ceramcoat, Vallejo, and Model Master Acryl.

Many brands of spray paint for modeling are available, including Model Master, Testors, and Scalecoat, along with popular general-purpose paints such as Krylon.

Model paints

Although two major model paint lines disappeared in recent years (Floquil and Polly Scale), there are still fine paints available (and many modelers probably have ample supplies of older paints still on hand).

Model paints fall into two broad categories: water-based (acrylics) and solvent-based. I use acrylics almost exclusively, and I highly recommend them for several reasons. First, they are much safer to use, without the worry of inhaling vapors from organic solvents. Second, after use, brushes and airbrushes can be cleaned with water instead of thinner. Third, acrylics work well.

Today's **acrylic paints** are much improved over the first modeling water-based paints that appeared in the 1980s. They cover well, readily adhere to most surfaces, can easily be applied by brush or airbrush, and are available in a tremendous variety of colors. Widely available acrylics designed for models include Badger Modelflex, Micro-Mark MicroLux, Model Master Acryl, and Vallejo, **2**.

Water-based craft paints, such as Delta Ceramcoat and Apple Barrel, are also handy for many modeling uses including detail and figure painting.

Spray paints (spray cans) are good for covering large surfaces quickly, **3**. Model spray paints include Scalecoat, Testors, and Model Master. You can also use general-purpose spray paints such as Krylon and other brands, which are available at hardware and home improvement stores. General-purpose paints work fine for most structure applications, but be aware that they may produce a thicker coat than most model paints. I like to use Krylon's clear matte and clear gloss sprays for applying quick clear coats to models.

Vapors from spray paints are harmful, so when using them—be sure to provide adequate ventilation: use them outside or in a vented spray booth. Don't just use them in a spare room. A rule of thumb is that if you can smell the paint, you need more ventilation.

Paint markers are another handy way of applying paint, **4**. Testors CreateFX line includes weathering colors as well as silver, gold, white, black, and other colors. Sharpie also offers a line of paint markers. These markers contain enamel paint and should also be used with proper ventilation. (Make sure to use the company's paint markers and not their permanent ink markers.)

Artist's tube acrylics and oils are useful for staining bare wood and for applying weathering washes on various surfaces, **4**. Black, burnt umber, burnt sienna, and raw sienna are all useful colors to have on hand.

Paints come in various sheens, from flat to semigloss and gloss. Most of your models will look better with flat finishes, so use flat colors if possible. If you're planning to apply decals to a model, use gloss paints. You can always add a clear overcoat to provide the finish that you need.

Brushes

You'll find a variety of brushes helpful for painting structures and other modeling projects, **5**. Buy good-quality brushes. They don't have to be the most expensive artist's brushes on the rack, but avoid the six-for-a-dollar discount brushes. A good brush, if cleaned well, will last for years.

Flat brushes in widths from ¼" to ¾" work well for finish painting and covering large surfaces. Finish brushes should be soft—synthetic and sable are ideal—to avoid leaving brush marks. Less-expensive ox- and camel-hair brushes are fine for painting rough surfaces, applying washes, weathering, and applying powdered chalk.

Small round brushes (the smaller the number, the finer the tip) can be used for painting details and tight areas. My favorite is the Model Master synthetic no. 0, which has a tip that's fine enough for most detail work, but large enough that it holds enough paint to not require constant reloading. I also have nos. 00, 1, and 2 round synthetic and sable brushes.

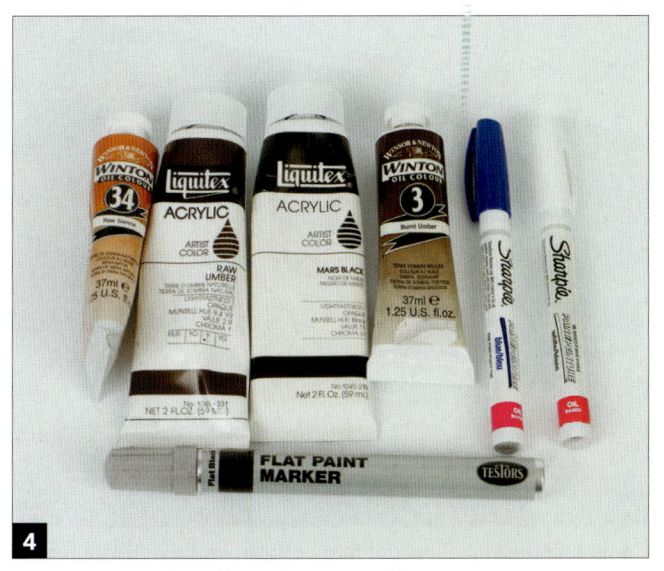

Using paint markers from Sharpie and Testors is an easy way to apply paint. Artist's acrylics and oils are useful for staining wood and weathering various surfaces.

You'll find uses for a variety of brush types and sizes. Wide, flat sable and synthetic brushes are good for weathering and adding finish coats to large surfaces. Small, round brushes are useful for detail painting, and stiff hog bristle brushes work well for chalks and drybrushing.

Stiff brushes, such as hog bristle, are great for many weathering applications, including drybrushing and applying chalk.

Cleaning brushes

A key to keeping brushes in good shape is proper cleaning. Start by wetting the brush, and then use a paper towel to remove excess water before each use. Doing this helps keep paint from drying and sticking to the bristles, which makes later cleanup easier.

After every use with acrylic paint, clean your brushes under running water, using a drop of dish detergent. Work the detergent into the bristles and then rinse until no signs of the color remain. Dry the brush with a paper towel, then reshape the brush tip, and store the brush upside-down in a cup or jar.

Do not simply swish the brush in water or thinner and dry it. Paint will remain among the bristles and cause the brush to lose its shape, with bristles splaying outward. Also, don't let your brushes sit in water or thinner. This will bend the bristles permanently and ruin the brush.

When you're done cleaning a brush, all traces of paint should be gone—you shouldn't be able to tell what color was just applied.

Painting techniques

Brush-painting plastic, resin, and metal surfaces is straightforward. Start by making sure the surface to be painted is clean and free of dust. Oils from your skin can keep acrylic paints from bonding to a model, especially on smooth surfaces. If you've handled a model often with bare hands, wash it with warm water and a drop of dish detergent. (Always wash resin surfaces.) Then rinse the model and allow it to air dry.

Thoroughly mix the paint by shaking or stirring. Stirring is a good first step if the paint has been sitting for awhile and the pigment has settled; then you can shake it to complete the mixing. Air is the enemy of water-based paint, so if a paint bottle will be open for more than a minute or two, use an eyedropper or pipette to transfer some paint to a palette or other temporary holder.

When opening a bottle of acrylic paint, you'll sometimes find a skin of dried paint atop the bottle opening or a ring of dried paint around the opening. Use a toothpick or tweezers to remove this, making sure it doesn't drop into the bottle. Likewise, before closing a bottle, make sure the lip of the bottle, its threads, and the cap are completely clean and free of paint. This not only makes the bottle easier to open next time, it keeps dried flakes from contaminating the paint.

When painting large surfaces, such as structure walls or roofs, use as wide a brush as practical. First, dip the brush in water and then wipe it off. This keeps paint from drying on the bristles and makes cleanup easier.

Dip the bristle tips in paint. Try to keep the paint on the lower third of the bristles. Start in one corner of the surface, applying the paint in smooth, even strokes, **6**. One or two brush strokes should do it—once the paint is smoothly applied, leave it alone: the paint will level as it dries. Continuing to brush the paint will leave stroke marks on the surface.

As you apply more paint, add it to a neighboring dry area, brushing it back toward the still-wet, most-recently painted area. This minimizes visible brush marks. Again, use only enough brush strokes to distribute the paint.

An advantage of painting structures is that most surfaces have some sort of texture, which can help hide brush marks. Keep brush strokes in the same direction as any marks on the surface: siding, corrugations, wall panels, and the horizontal lines of bricks and concrete blocks.

6 Use as wide a brush as practical when painting large surfaces. Brush the paint on in smooth, even strokes.

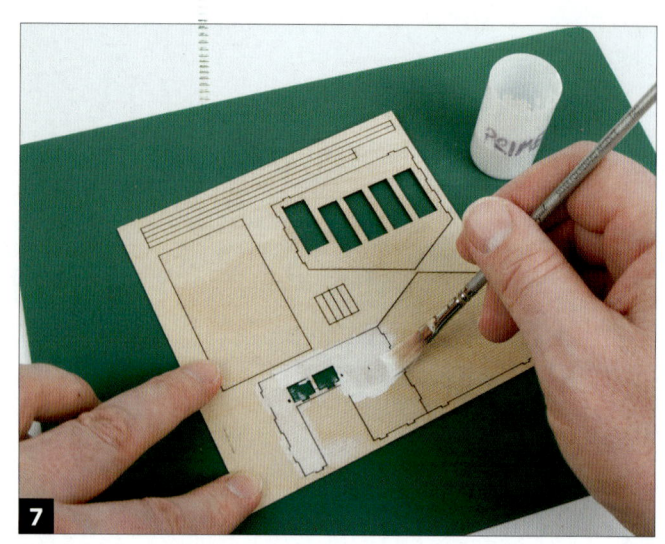

7 Common household interior latex primer works well as a first coat for wood parts. This is the GC Laser depot kit from chapter 2.

8 After priming both sides of the parts sheet, I applied the finish coat of maroon paint. It took two coats to cover completely.

9 A foam brush works well for trim and long strip material when you're trying to cover all faces of the material. Press the brush to the paint and then dab along the material.

Allow the paint to dry completely. With acrylics, you can use a hair dryer to speed up the drying process. Let the paint dry on its own for a minute to level, then pass the hair dryer over the surface for a minute or two to help cure the paint, and you're ready for the next coat.

If the paint color is close to that of the building's surface, you might be able to get by with just one finish coat. Darker paints also tend to cover better with one coat. Look at the model under good lighting to see that the paint color is even and that no sign of the original surface shows through. Make sure all corners and crevices have been coated.

If you need a second coat, follow the same process as painting the first one. The second coat can often be lighter. Check the model again for complete coverage.

It can be difficult to get even coverage of many light colors (yellow, white, orange, bright red) with a brush, especially over dark or contrasting surfaces. Starting with a primer coat of light gray can help. However, your best bet for smooth results with light colors is usually to either airbrush or use a spray can.

Painting and staining wood

Finishing wood requires a slightly different approach when compared to plastic. Wood is porous and will absorb paint quickly. If you try to apply a thin coat, it will dry before it has a chance to level. Because wood has a grain, it will often show through the paint, as different areas of the wood absorb the paint at different rates. Wood can also warp and expand when painted—the thinner the sheet, the more this occurs.

For large surfaces, such as structure walls and roofs, start with a coat of primer, **7**. Common household latex

10 You can use thinned acrylic paint for staining wood, as on this scribed floor. This is a black wash; various shades of brown are also effective.

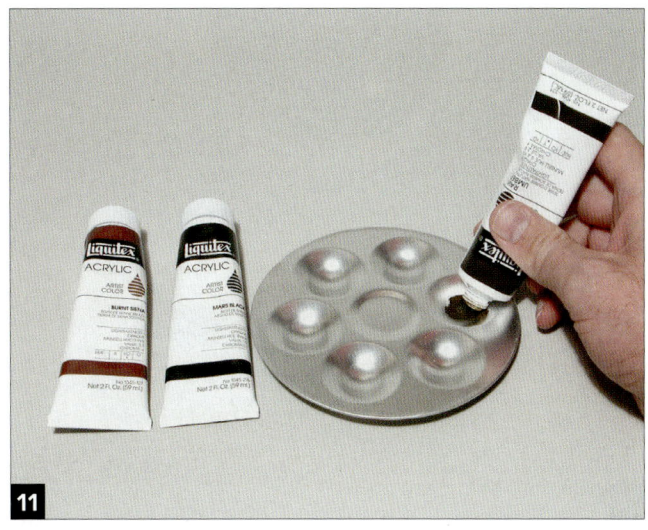

11 Artist's tube acrylics work well for creating the effect of weathered wood. Squeeze several colors into an aluminum palette and then add water.

12 Brush on the stain in the direction of the siding or grain.

13 You can add highlights to individual boards, and add successively darker layers of stain to any part of the wall.

primer is designed for this purpose, and it works very well on models. I had a gallon can handy from another project, so once it was thoroughly mixed, I transferred some into a spare container (an old film canister) to make it handier for modeling. Latex primer is thicker than standard model paint. It covers very well, it's easy to brush, it seals the wood, and it provides a uniform base for the finish color, **8**.

To minimize the effects of warping, paint both sides of any sheet material. This also helps minimize shrinking and expansion from humidity and moisture after the structure is completed.

If wood grain or fuzz is still visible after priming, you can lightly sand the areas with fine (440-grit or finer) sandpaper and then reprime the areas that were sanded. Use a sanding stick for tight areas or along texture lines, such as clapboard.

Once the wood is primed, you can use the same painting techniques as done with plastic. Brush-painting, airbrushing, and spray painting all work well.

For fine parts, such as thin trim boards, you can use a small brush, but this can be time consuming if there's a lot of material. You can also use a foam brush by picking up paint with the end of the brush and dabbing it on the parts, **9**.

You can stain wood to replicate the effect of bare, weathered wood. Testors CreateFX line of enamel stains can be used for this. However, I usually just mix my own stains and washes, which can be made in various colors.

Bare wood exposed to the elements can take on a number of shades depending upon the type of wood, how long it has been outside, how much moisture it is exposed to, and whether it was treated with creosote or something else. Colors can include a range from light to dark gray and brown, as well as green and rust colors.

14
To simulate peeling paint, brush patches of rubber cement on a stained wood wall.

15
Paint the wall, and when the paint dries, use a pencil eraser to scrub off the patches of cement.

16
The finished wall will look like it's in need of a fresh paint job. The more you rub with the eraser, the more weathered the wall will appear.

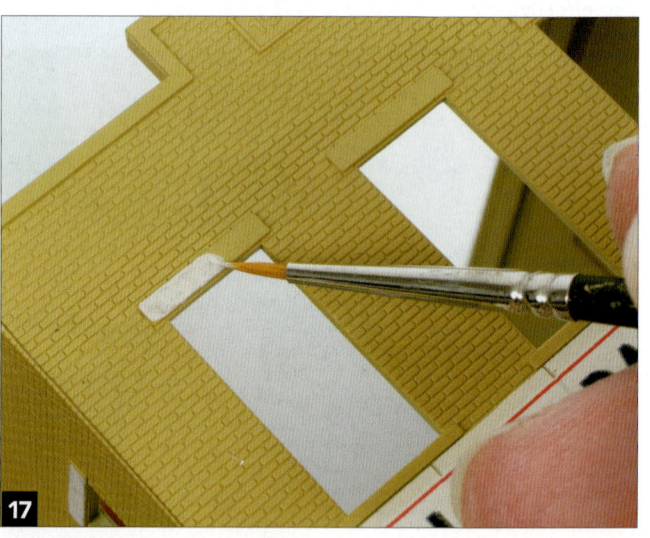

17
For raised surfaces, such as this window header, working slowly, use the side of the brush to dab and push paint to the edges.

To duplicate this on a model, start by determining the color you want to capture. Acrylic model paints work well for making stain—start with a mix of about 1 part paint to 10 parts water (or the thinner for that brand of paint), **10**.

You can also use artist's tube acrylics. My favorite colors for stain are black for any shade of gray, and raw sienna, burnt sienna, and burnt umber for various shades of brown. Squeeze a bit of each color into one recess in an aluminum palette and then add water, **11**. Use a brush to apply the stain (first try it on a scrap piece to check the color), **12**.

Let the stain dry completely. You can then add another coat to darken the effect or highlight individual boards, which helps sheet material look more realistic, **13**.

Another popular stain mix is India ink and alcohol. Fill a 1- or 2-ounce bottle with common rubbing alcohol and then add a few drops of India ink. Test it on a scrap piece and add more ink if needed.

It's a good idea to stain siding and trim pieces before assembly, as glue will keep stain from penetrating the wood. You can build up effects with multiple coats. Start with a lighter color or mix and then follow with an additional coat of stain, building up the color gradually. Let the piece dry completely before evaluating the color—when dry, the wood will usually appear lighter than when the stain was first applied.

Sheet material will warp when the stain is applied. Staining both sides (or painting the back side with primer) helps reduce the warping. The warping also usually lessens as the piece dries. Let stained wood pieces dry thoroughly before continuing to assemble the kit or gluing pieces together.

Simulating peeling paint is another effect that you can show on wood structures. Start by staining the walls light to medium gray and then assemble the structure. Use a fine brush to apply rubber cement as a mask to

18 On recessed surfaces, such as this window frame, ease the paint toward the raised surface with the brush angled downward, so only the bristle tips contact the neighboring ridge.

19 Paint markers, such as this white marker from Sharpie, can also be used to color trim and details.

20 Cut masking tape on a piece of glass using a straightedge to get a clean edge.

21 Use multiple pieces of tape to mask the surface. Follow lines on the model surface whenever possible.

small areas along the siding, **14**. Brush-paint or airbrush the walls, and then as soon as the paint dries, rub away the rubber cement with an eraser to leave patches of bare wood showing through the paint, **15**. You can vary this effect from a few small patches to large areas of peeling paint, **16**.

Detail painting

A lot of details require painting, including window frames, door frames, trim, vents, and other small parts. Whenever possible, paint details separately before adding them to a model. You can stick small pieces to a piece of tape as a holder to make the details easier to paint.

Many kits—especially injection-molded styrene models—have details molded in place. Paint the main walls first and then proceed to the details. Use a small brush (generally no. 0 or smaller), but one that's as large as practical. Dip just the tips of the bristles in the paint and carefully paint the detail, **17**.

Use the shape of the details to your advantage when painting. For raised surfaces, such as window ledges, dab the brush with the paint on the surface to the edge. Let the surface tension of the paint keep it from flowing to a neighboring surface. Another trick is to use the side of the brush to dab paint on raised surfaces.

For recessed areas, work the paint slowly to the nearest raised surface, **18**. Keep the brush angled downward so that only the tips of the bristles contact the raised area, which keeps paint in the recessed area.

Paint markers are another choice for details and trim, **19**. The markers don't offer as fine control as a brush, but they are quick and easy to use. As with the window frames seen in the photo, you can get most of the areas covered with

65

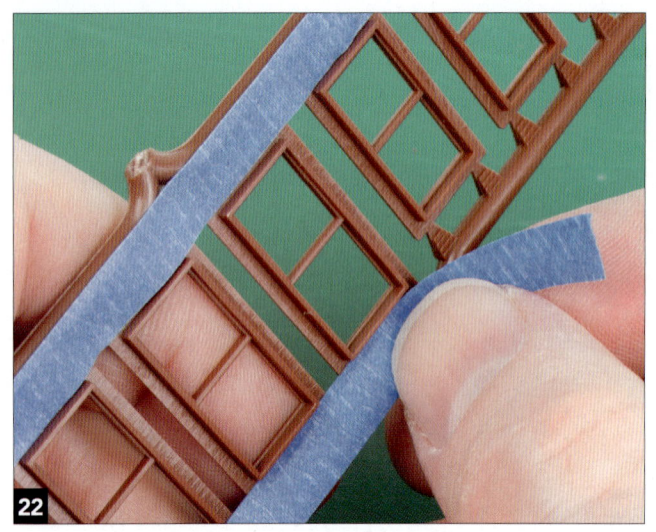

22 Also, be sure to mask gluing surfaces on detail items like these window frames.

23 Burnish the tape edges firmly to the surface with your fingernail or a piece of wood (don't use a metal tool).

24 Peeling the tape back at a sharp angle minimizes stress on the initial paint coat. The separation line on this City Classics store is clean and well defined.

25 With a spray can, make quick, overlapping passes, starting and stopping the spray off the edge of the model. Two light coats are better than one heavy coat.

the marker, and then finish tight areas with a brush.

If you accidentally get paint on a neighboring surface, don't worry. Let the paint dry, and then either carefully scrape it off with the tip of a no. 11 knife blade or use a fine-tip brush to touch up the neighboring surface.

Masking

Multicolor paint schemes sometimes require masking to get a precise line between the colors. You can mask models whether you are brush-painting, airbrushing, or using spray cans. In general, for multicolor schemes, start painting with the lightest color (or a primer) and then add progressively darker colors.

You can safely mask as soon as the base color has set. For acrylics, let the paint dry, use a hair dryer on it for a minute, and you're ready to mask. As long as the paint has been properly applied, masking tape will not pull the paint up when it's removed.

My favorite tape for masking is 3M blue painter's tape. It's easy to cut and place, adheres well, flexes over details, and is easy to remove. Standard masking tape also works well, but it has stronger adhesive. Regular transparent tape can also be used for flat surfaces without large obstructions.

Cutting the masking tape on a piece of glass provides a clean, sharp edge, and also allows you to trim the tape to whatever width or shape you need, **20**. Position the tape on the model, following markings or ridges on the surface if possible, **21**. Use tweezers to get tape into tight areas. If you're brush-painting, you only need tape next to the mask line, but if using a spray can or airbrush, cover the entire model. When airbrushing detail items (such as window frames on a sprue), mask the gluing edges before painting, **22**.

Burnish the tape edges along the mask line, rubbing them firmly to the

26 An airbrush provides the best control. The paint should go on wet, and each pass should overlap the previous one. Use a hair dryer to dry the paint, then proceed with the next coat.

27 Touch a brush dampened with mineral spirits to artist's oil color and then streak the brush down the surface (in this case, rust colors down a silver simulated-metal roof).

28 To drybrush, start by dipping the tips of bristles of a stiff brush in paint and wipe most of the paint off on a paper towel.

29 Streak the nearly dry brush across the model. Drybrushing can simulate many effects. Here, I used the structure color to simulate faded, peeling lettering.

surface to ensure that paint won't seep under the edge, **23**. You can use the back of your fingernail or the end of a wood stick, being careful not to scratch the exposed surface.

Apply the second color. Whether airbrushing, brush-painting, or using a spray can, applying an initial light coat of paint helps seal the tape edge. If brush-painting, keep brush strokes parallel to the tape edge to minimize the chances of paint bleeding and excessive paint buildup along the edge.

Remove the masking tape when the second color is dry. Pulling the tape sharply back over itself minimizes the stress on the base coat and limits the chances of unintentionally peeling off any paint, **24**. If any paint did seep under the tape edge, just touch up the area with a brush.

Spray painting

The easiest way to get an even paint coat on a large surface—especially a smooth one—is by using a spray can or airbrushing. These are also the best ways to apply a clear coat on any surface.

Spray cans are handy, especially for large structures and walls, but be sure to use them only in a vented spray booth or outdoors, as the solvent vapors are harmful. Spray cans need to be warm (at least normal room temperature) to work well. Placing the can in a bowl or pan of warm (not hot) water for five minutes helps the paint mix and flow more readily.

Shake the can vigorously for at least a minute to thoroughly mix the paint. Test the paint by spraying a test pattern on a scrap of cardboard, making sure the paint comes out evenly with no spatters.

With most spray cans, the paint comes out quickly. Hold the can 6"–12" above the model surface. Begin spraying off to one side and then move the can steadily across the model, stopping off the other edge, **25**.

Painting brick and mortar

Look at brick buildings in the real world, and you'll find an infinite variety of brick colors, mortar colors, paint, and weathering effects. Shades of dark red and brown are most common for brick, but many shades of cream and buff/yellow are also out there as well. When it comes to mortar, too many modelers reach for white paint—medium to dark gray is actually the most common mortar color, and mortar often has brick color mixed in.

Some structures use bricks of one color, while others have individual bricks that range widely in appearance, **1**. Walls that have been painted are uniform in color. Many walls were painted with signs, and the lettering of early 20th century signs can still be found on some buildings. (More on signs in chapter 7.)

There are a number of methods of re-creating brick. For a basic brick color, almost any shade of boxcar red, maroon, tuscan, or mineral brown serves as a good starting point.

One way to add mortar color to a brick wall is with a wash. Paint the wall with the brick color and then mix a wash of the mortar color. For the building in photo **2** (Nelson Appliance building seen in chapter 5), I used a 2:1 mix of light gray and boxcar red, and then thinned that mix about 8:1 with water. Apply the wash, making sure the wall is flat so the wash flows evenly. The wash will settle into the mortar lines and will also tone down the color of the brick surface.

This effect can vary widely, depending upon the size of the bricks and the depth and width of the mortar lines, so it's a good idea to test the wash on an obscure place. Let the wash dry thoroughly before turning the structure to do another side.

In another painting method, you start by painting the wall the mortar color and then brush on the brick color, **3**. Use a wide, flat brush, and make sure to dab the paint on the brick surface instead of using traditional brush coats.

You could also start with a wall painted the brick color and then paint it with mortar color and—while the paint is still wet—wipe it off, **4**. This leaves the mortar color in the lines. This older technique is messy, and other than on very small structures, I tend to use the other methods more often.

With any of these techniques, you can add the appearance of other-colored bricks by simply brushing some bricks with different colors, **5**. Put a few drops of two or three other colors on a piece of scrap and use a fine-point brush to paint the bricks. You can also use artist's colored pencils for this.

When you're finished, give the structure a light coat of clear flat finish for a uniform sheen.

1 Brick varies widely in appearance. The building at left has polished white brick on the front, the middle building has cream-colored brick on the front with red on the side (with remnants of old painted signs), and the building at right has a red front with cream sides.

2 You can add mortar color by spreading a wash across the entire wall. The wash settles in the mortar lines (just make sure the wall is level).

3 To color the mortar you can paint the wall the mortar color and then dab the brick color to the wall with a wide, flat brush.

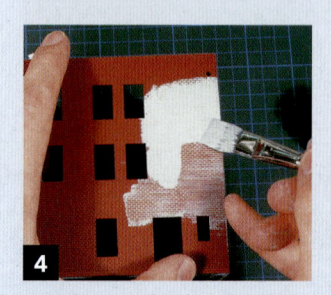

4 Another method is to brush mortar-colored paint on the surface, and then wipe it off, which leaves the mortar color in the grooves.

5 Use a brush or colored pencil to highlight individual bricks with different colors.

Continue by slightly overlapping each pass.

Don't try to cover a model in one coat—two or three lighter coats provides better results. Allow each coat to dry thoroughly before applying the next one (check instructions on the can for curing time and other information). Use short bursts to get paint into crevices, inside corners, and other tight areas.

When you're done painting, tip the can upside-down and spray until paint stops coming out. This ensures that the nozzle and delivery tube stay clean and clear.

Spray cans work well for applying clear coats. My favorites for this are Krylon's clear gloss and clear matte

You can effectively create general rust, grime, and dust effects with powdered chalk.

Chalks can be also used on wood surfaces. Here, I added wheel marks on the truck-bay floor of the base of a grain elevator.

Work gray powdered chalk into the surface of a brick wall, making sure the mortar lines are covered.

Wipe off the surface to leave the chalk settled in the mortar lines. Add a light clear coat to seal it.

finishes and Model Master clear semigloss finish. Again, use them only in a well-ventilated area.

Airbrushing

Although not a necessity, an airbrush is a handy tool for painting structures. I usually reach for my airbrush if I'm painting a large, smooth area (especially if a light color is involved) or a collection of details with multiple surfaces to cover (such as a group of window frames).

If you decide to invest in an airbrush, here are some hints to get you going:

• A simple external-mix, single-action airbrush will handle most modeling jobs, and one is easy to learn to use. Practice your techniques on scrap pieces before attempting to paint an actual model.

• Acrylic paints work well in airbrushes, but many require thinning 10 to 20 percent with water or a paint brand's respective thinner, and they usually spray well at 15–20 psi.

• As with a paintbrush, clean your airbrush thoroughly after each use. Disassemble the nozzle and other parts to remove all traces of paint.

• Invest in a permanent air source, such as a small air compressor. You can use cans of propellant, but they are expensive, don't last long, and are difficult to control.

• Only airbrush models in a spray booth. Make sure the booth is vented to the outdoors if you are using solvent-based paints because, while a filtered booth will remove paint particulates, the filter cannot remove harmful solvent vapors.

When airbrushing, the paint should go on wet, and it will usually dry within a couple of seconds. Overlap each pass slightly, **26**. After each coat, dry the paint for a minute with a hair dryer and then add additional coats as needed.

Weathering

Real buildings don't remain freshly painted for long. Sun and rain cause

34 Rubbing the surface with a wire brush creates light, subtle marks that resemble wood grain showing through the paint.

35 Dragging a razor saw across individual boards leaves deeper grain marks and reveals underlying paint colors.

36 Lifting up a few individual boards with a hobby knife helps give the impression that the wall was not molded as a single piece.

37 The finished effect is that of a worn, weatherbeaten wall of an older building.

paint to fade and peel, brick oxidizes, painted-on signs fade and peel, metal siding and roofs rust, and other roofs fade and wear. We've already looked at several weathering methods when staining wood and creating peeled-paint effects.

A variation on washes uses artist's oil colors and mineral spirits to create streaked, rusty, and weathered effects. Squeeze dabs of several colors (black, burnt sienna, raw sienna) into an aluminum palette. Dip the brush in mineral spirits and then touch it to one of the colors and streak the brush downward, **27**. You can mix the colors and vary the intensity by how damp the brush is. If you don't like an effect, wipe it off with mineral spirits and start over.

Another use of washes is to simulate mortar on brick (see "Painting brick and mortar" on page 68 for details).

Drybrushing is done by dipping the tips of stiff brush bristles in paint, wiping most of the paint off on a paper towel, and then streaking the brush across the model, **28**. Drybrushing can create a variety of effects, including rust streaks, soot, and peeling paint, **29**.

Weathering with chalk

Powdered chalks are available in weathering colors (black, gray, brown, and rust) from AIM, Bar Mills, Bragdon, and others. You can also make your own by scraping sticks of artist's pastel chalks, which are available in a variety of colors at craft stores.

An advantage of chalks is that the effects are largely reversible; if you don't like an effect, wipe the chalk off the surface with a damp cloth. If a model is going to be handled, it's a good idea to seal the chalk with a coat of flat clear.

The key to achieving good effects with chalk is to apply them to a dead-flat surface—glossy finishes won't hold the chalk, and it will blow away when a clear overcoat is applied. If the model has been painted with gloss or semigloss paint, give it a light coat of clear flat before adding chalk.

Painting plaster

Some structure kits, notably those from Banta Modelworks, C. C. Crow, and Downtown Deco—along with details from AIM Products, Woodland Scenics, and others—are cast in various types of plaster.

Painting plaster is not difficult. As with other materials, you can use a brush, spray can, or airbrush. Because plaster is porous, it will drink in paint like a sponge. For small parts and buildings, this isn't a big concern. For larger projects, if you give the structure or component a coat of clear flat finish, it helps seal it prior to painting.

Plaster's porous surface usually yields a flat finish regardless of the type of paint used, and it also means plaster can easily be stained to various effects with thinned acrylic paint. This lends itself well to representing brick, stone, and other masonry.

A brush works well for painting plaster. Be sure to work the paint into all the cracks and crevices. Applying an initial clear coat will keep the plaster from absorbing as much of the finish coat of paint.

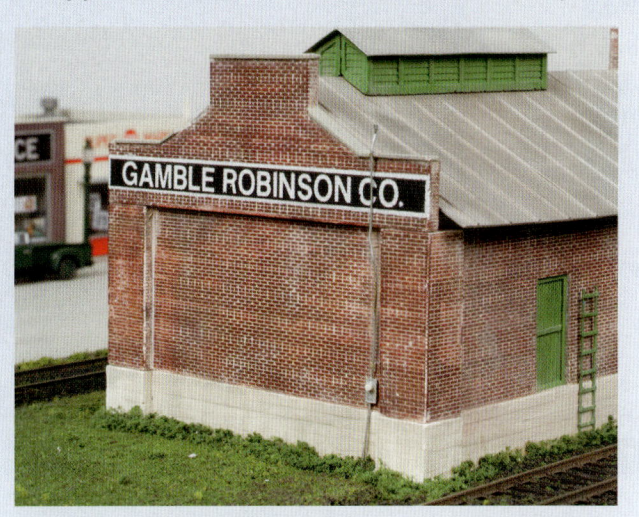

This plaster apple warehouse kit from C. C. Crow was painted using the dabbing technique, with the original plaster color in the mortar joints. The foundation was stained an aged concrete color. George Sebastian-Coleman did the modeling. Chapter 7 shows how to make the painted-on sign using dry transfer lettering.

Chalks are great for creating sooty appearances around chimneys and smokestacks and for producing grime, rust, and grunge effects on roofs, walls, and details, **30**. Apply powdered chalk with a soft brush for adding overall soot and dust effects, or use a stiff brush if you want to work it into the surface, which you can do if you want a streaked or ground-in effect, **31**.

Seal chalk with a light coat of clear flat from an airbrush or spray can. (I like Krylon's clear matte or Model Master clear semigloss or flat.) If some of the effect disappears when the clear coat dries, add more chalk and repeat the process. Be sure to mask windows when adding clear coats.

Chalks work well for simulating mortar on brick surfaces, **32**. Use a soft brush to work the chalk across the surface, where it tends to settle in the mortar cracks. Then use a brush or soft cloth to remove most of the chalk from the surface, **33**. Seal the chalk with a clear coat. As when using washes for this, the effects will vary depending upon the type and texture of the brick and the depth of the mortar lines.

Other weathering techniques

Along with washes, drybrushing, and chalks, you can use various tools to inflict "damage" and layer weathering effects. I'll give some examples using a Walthers HO grain elevator, an injection-molded styrene kit with molded clapboard siding that was molded red. First, I spray-painted it boxcar red, added dry transfer lettering (see chapter 7), drybrushed the lettering to make it look faded, and then added a flat clear coat. I wanted the model to represent an older elevator but one that was still in service in the 1960s period that I model.

Using a wire brush, I scraped the model along the clapboard lines, **34**. This created a subtle effect of having some wood grain show through the paint, and if done with enough force, it can look like lightly peeling paint.

Moving to a more serious tool, I used a razor saw to make deeper lines that simulated grain and peeling paint, **35**. I tried to keep this effect to individual boards. This look can be enhanced if you first paint the model dark gray or grimy black before applying the finish color, as you'll have more varied colors showing through.

I finished by using a no. 17 hobby blade to lift up parts of individual boards on the surface, **36**. You can vary this effect depending upon how weather-beaten you want a structure to appear, **37**. The finished structure appears in chapter 8.

These techniques work on wood structures as well. When doing this on wood, start by staining the wood before applying the final colors.

CHAPTER SEVEN

Signs

Signs on these buildings include painted-on (dry transfers used as masks) on the upper side wall, a decal made from a photograph (Occident Flour), decal (barber shop) and printed signs (shoe store) from graphic design programs, and three-dimensional lettering from a swizzle stick (Webster's on the shoe store), and specialty (the barber pole).

Nothing gives a structure some personality as signs do. A combination of local business names, national brand logos, store chains, and custom-made businesses will make your kit-built models unique when compared to the thousands of otherwise identical structures on layouts across the country, **1**.

2 Decal alphabets, decal signs, and printed signs are available from Blair Line, JL Innovative Design, Microscale, City Classics, and others.

3 Slater's makes injection-molded styrene letters in a variety of sizes (shown here in 3mm and 6mm). The larger letters are ½" signboard letters from an office supply store.

4 Craft stores sell raised plastic and foam letters in many styles. Thickers is one brand, which is made by American Crafts.

5 Sign sources can include old road maps, matchbooks, advertising pieces, photos, and various other materials.

Signs

You can customize a building with signs to represent those on specific prototype structures from any era, and you can also come up with your own business and industry names to immortalize friends and family.

Many signs simply display the name of a business, while others include graphics, such as a corporate logo or symbol, together with lettering.

Prototype structure signs include
- flat boards attached to a wall
- three-dimensional lettering and graphics
- hanging signs (especially popular on buildings through the 1970s)
- signs painted directly on structures

Structures—especially large ones—often served as billboards, with large advertisements painted directly on the walls. These ads sometimes reflected products related to the building or a business in it. The painted-on signs were very popular in the early 1900s, and many signs of that period lasted late into the 20th century (and you'll still find some around today), often showing products that are no longer available for a business that has long since vacated the building.

There are two keys to making realistic signs. The first is the lettering and graphics: Make sure any logos and lettering fonts are accurate for the era you are modeling. The second key is that the signs should be applied in a realistic manner.

Model manufacturers produce a large variety of signs, **2**. Printed paper signs and decal signs of many real and fictional companies and logos are available from Bar Mills, Blair Line, City Classics, JL Innovative Design, Microscale, and others. Bar Mills and Blair Line both offer billboard and sign kits with laser-cut lettering and logos that can easily be applied to structures.

Individual plastic letters are available in sizes from 2mm and 3mm to 16mm from Slater's, and office supply dealers have these in ½" and larger sizes as well, **3**. Raised three-dimensional craft

73

6 The May Brothers sign is simply white letters laid over a black rectangle in Photoshop and sized to fit the available space on the building.

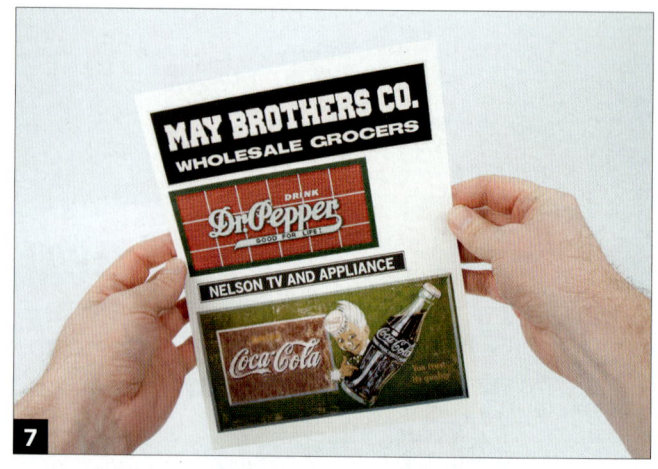

7 I printed the May Brothers sign on white decal paper, together with the sign for an appliance store and two large beverage billboards that I thought might work on building walls.

8 Cut the decal from the sheet. A clear drafting triangle allows you to see exactly where the edge of the graphic is located.

9 Dip the decal in water for about 15 seconds. Long, narrow decals like this one tend to curl initially when they hit the water.

lettering (foam and plastic) in a variety of styles and sizes can be found at stores such as Michaels and Hobby Lobby, **4**. You can see these in use on the scratchbuilt branch house in chapter 4.

Decal and dry-transfer alphabet and number sets in many style, sizes, and colors are made by Clover House, Microscale, Woodland Scenics, and others. They allow you to customize building signs, and you can combine them with logos and graphics to make unique signs.

The best sources for signs may be from nonconventional sources. With the high quality of today's computer printers and the resources available through the Internet, almost anything that you can find a photo of (or take a photo of) can be turned into a sign for a model. For the last 25 years, I've made a habit of photographing building signs of all types—hanging, mounted, and painted on—just in case I found a need for it on a model at some point. The Internet is a treasure trove of images, with many sites devoted to signs and building photos.

Keep your eyes open for items that use a company logo and lettering, such as company letterhead, envelopes, books, pamphlets, packaging, advertising, calendars, matchbooks, gas company road maps, drink coasters, stir sticks, and promotional items, **5**. Antique stores and eBay are good places to search.

Regarding copyright and trademark use, you are generally free to use images and logos from the Internet and other sources for your own use, such as making signs for your structures. However, you do not have the right to distribute others' photos or corporate logos (which are trademarked) to anyone else without the owners' permission. Keep in mind that these restrictions apply whether or not you charge money for them.

Computer manipulation

A computer is a valuable tool in making and customizing model signs. Chapter 5 showed how you can design boxes, cases, walls, doors, and other interior details. You can follow the

10 Remove the decal from water and place it on a paper towel. Straighten the decal if necessary.

11 Begin sliding the decal off the paper. Hold one end in place and then carefully slide the backing paper away.

12 Add setting solution on the top and edges of the decal, being careful not to bump the decal out of alignment.

13 The May Brothers decal was too large to apply at once, so I cut it into pieces to fit between and atop the vertical pilasters.

same basic techniques in making signs. (And chapter 8 has more details on making entire structure walls this way).

You can make a basic sign by simply adding lettering over a plain or colored background. I use Adobe Photoshop Elements, but you can use almost any graphics or photo program. You can add trim lines, outlines, and logos as needed.

Measure your structure and make the sign background the appropriate size. Your computer should have a collection of fonts (lettering styles), but you can also download fonts from sites such as dafont.com and fontspace.com. Many are free (or free for noncommercial use such as on your layout). Study lettering styles from the era you're modeling. A majority of fonts available today have been created in the past few years—and look very modern—meaning they would not be appropriate for the steam and early diesel eras.

Experiment with various lettering sizes and arrangements until you find something that works for your structure. Photo **6** shows the sign I designed for the large grocery wholesaler shown in chapter 3. You can print the resulting sign or signs on plain paper, cardstock, matte photo paper, or decal paper (white or clear). I've had good luck with 8½" x 11" inkjet decal sheets from www.decalpaper.com; other sites also offer plain decal paper.

For the May Brothers sign, I measured the space on the structure (three modular building panels wide and one short story tall) and then set that size as a black rectangle. I tried various fonts and sizes—test-printing several on paper and taping them to the structure to check—until I found one that I liked.

When printing out signs, I try to group as many as possible on a single sheet of photo paper or decal paper to conserve materials, **7**. You can also resize signs and print them out in multiple sizes to provide options for finding the one that fits best.

Applying decals
Water-slide decals are available from Microscale, and many manufacturers include decals in their kits as well.

14 Lightly poke any trapped air bubbles or pockets with the tip of a hobby knife.

15 Reapply setting solution after poking air bubbles. You may have to repeat these steps, depending on the surface.

16 Use a fine brush and matching paint to touch up any areas that weren't covered by the decal, such as the side of this pilaster between decal sections.

17 Trace the dry transfer lettering to determine exactly how much space it will take up. The outside lines show the extreme edges of the elevator wall.

The techniques for applying decals are the same whether using commercial decals or your own. A key to successful application is applying decals to surfaces painted with gloss or semigloss paint. Decals don't adhere well to flat paint, and as a result, small trapped air pockets will appear under the decal (called *silvering*) and be visible under any clear film. If applying decals to a flat surface, add a clear gloss coat before applying decals.

If you've made your own decals with an inkjet printer, give the decal sheet two coats of clear gloss finish. I simply spray on Krylon clear gloss. This seals the ink and keeps it from running when the decal is dipped in water.

Start by trimming the decal as close as possible to the lettering or design. Use small scissors or a sharp hobby knife on a clean self-healing cutting mat, **8**. Dip the decal in a shallow dish of water, **9**. Always use distilled water for decaling—tap water often leaves mineral stains on model surfaces when it evaporates. Leave the decal in the water for about 15 seconds and then set it on a paper towel for a minute or so, **10**. If the decal curls, straighten it out after removing it from the water. As the decal sits, the backing glue loosens.

There are two types of decal setting solution: weak and strong. Weak solution (such as Microscale Micro Set) begins to soften a decal, but not enough that it can't still be handled. Strong solutions (Microscale Micro Sol or Walthers Solvaset) soften a decal more, which allows it to form itself around surface details and effectively bond to the surface.

Use a brush to apply a puddle of weak setting solution to the surface where the decal will be placed. Start sliding the decal off of the paper, keeping it aligned. For larger decals, use a finger or toothpick to hold a corner of it while sliding the paper away, **11**.

Straighten and position the decal with a toothpick or paintbrush (don't use tweezers or anything metal),

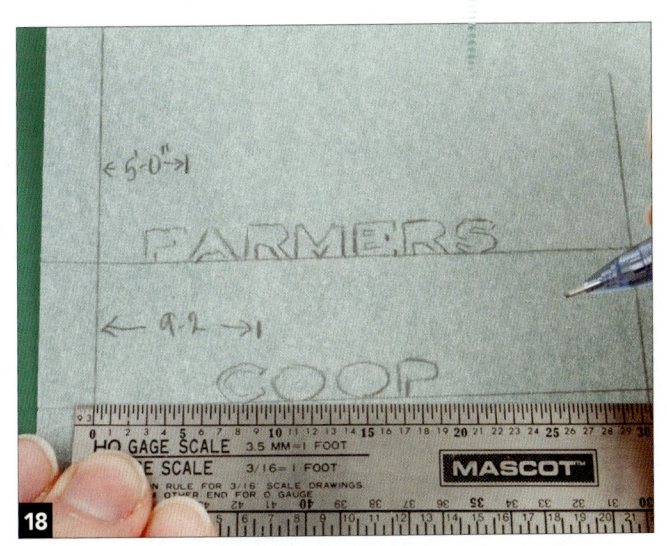

18 Comparing the lettering to the available space—in this case, the wall width—showed that I had to start the top line 5'-0" from the edge and the bottom line 9'-2" from the edge.

19 Carefully position the transfer sheet so the letter is aligned. Burnish the letter with moderate pressure until the letter is transferred.

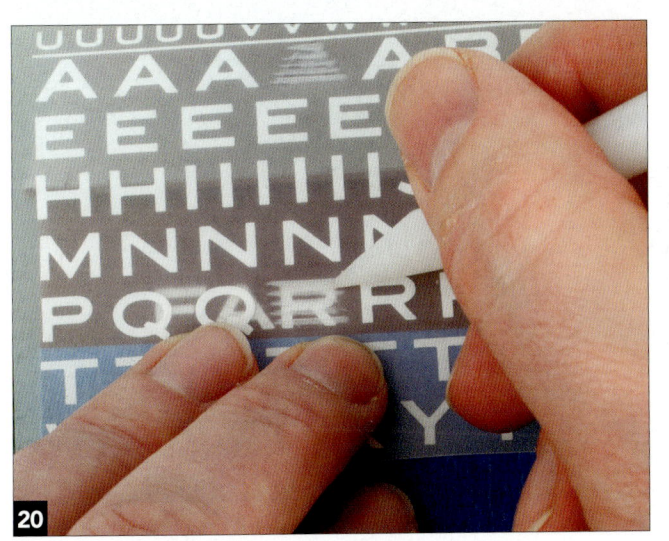

20 The letter changes appearance when it transfers. Finish with heavier pressure to secure it to the model.

21 Stores and businesses of all types had projecting signs. Many include logos and lettering for national brands or chains, often with the local business name added.

adding water to it if it sticks. Once the decal is in position, let it sit for a few minutes so it begins to adhere, and then use a brush to add strong setting solution on the decal's surface and around the edge, **12**.

Once you apply the strong setting solution, leave the decal alone until it dries—if you touch it now, you risk tearing it. The decal may wrinkle until it dries—this is normal. When it's dry, the decal will form itself to structure details, and any clear areas of the decal should blend into the painted surface.

You can apply large decals in several sections. Use surface divisions when doing this (such as the pilasters on the May Brothers building in photo **13**). Be sure to keep the decals aligned while applying them.

Once the decal dries completely, check for any places where it didn't adhere to the surface. These will show as bubbles or silvery areas, and they're more likely to appear around details in the surface. Poke the areas lightly with a sharp hobby knife and reapply setting solution, **14** and **15**. You may have to repeat the process multiple times, especially on rough, corrugated, or brick surfaces.

Use paint and a small brush to touch up any areas that need it, such as around edges of details or gaps where decals were applied in sections, **16**. When everything looks good, spray on a flat or semigloss clear coat to seal the decals. This helps hide clear decal film, hides the decal edges, and gives the entire model a uniform finish.

Dry transfers
Most dry transfers, or rub-ons, are alphabet and number sets, and they're available in many sizes, styles, and colors. An advantage of using dry transfers is that there's no carrier film to hide as with decals, and they can be applied to flat or gloss finishes. Dry transfers are burnished from their carrier sheet directly onto a model.

22 Print signs on matte photo paper. I printed these together with other building signs and some brick walls.

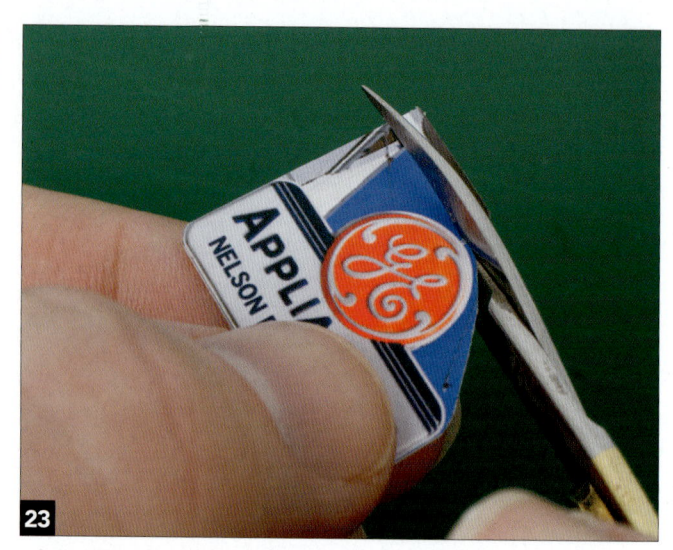

23 After adhering the sign to double-sided mounting paper, trim the sign to size with scissors or a hobby knife.

24 Trace the sign onto plastic as a guide and trim the plastic base to size with a hobby knife and files.

25 Then use a file or sand all the edges until they are smooth.

I do a bit of planning to make sure lettering fits and will be spaced properly when applied. I use see-through tracing paper to sketch the lettering, as with the FARMERS COOP lettering on the grain elevator in photo **17**. Once the lettering is traced on the paper, measure the length of each word and compare it to the available space to figure out where the lettering needs to start and stop on the actual structure, **18**.

Hold the transfer sheet securely on the model surface, **19**. Follow a line to make sure the lettering is horizontal. For this grain elevator, the clapboard siding provides a guide, and a piece of masking tape (also marked with the starting point) also helps. Once the first letter is in position, burnish it in place. I use a Teflon burnishing tool from Woodland Scenics, but you can also use a pencil. Go back and forth with moderate pressure in the direction of any surface details such as siding. When the letter has transferred, the color will change, **20**. Go back over the letter with heavier pressure to fully secure it to the model surface.

Continue the process with each letter, checking the alignment and spacing as you go. If a letter breaks or doesn't transfer properly, scrape it away and try again. (You can see the finished building in chapter 9.)

Hanging signs

Projecting signs—horizontal hanging signs and vertical signs mounted directly to structures—were common on retail storefront buildings through the 1970s, and many can still be found today. Many are flat sheet metal, illuminated by separate bulbs above or below the sign. Neon lighting was very popular through the mid-1900s, with tubes shaped to duplicate the lettering on the sign. Beginning in the mid-1900s, signs with translucent faces became common, illuminated by internal lamps or tubes, **21**.

Many national and regional chains and brands could be found on these signs, often with lettering for the individual store or business name. This was, and is, true for beer, soda, appliances, drug stores, grocery chains, and many other businesses.

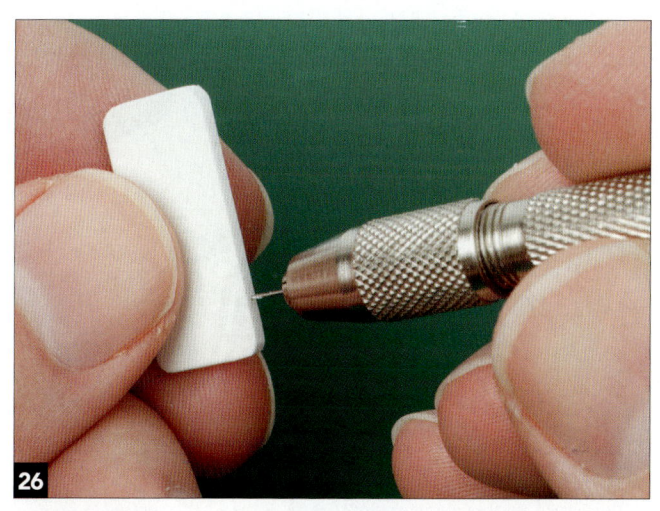

26 Drill mounting holes for the eye bolts or mounting rods in the edge of the styrene signboard.

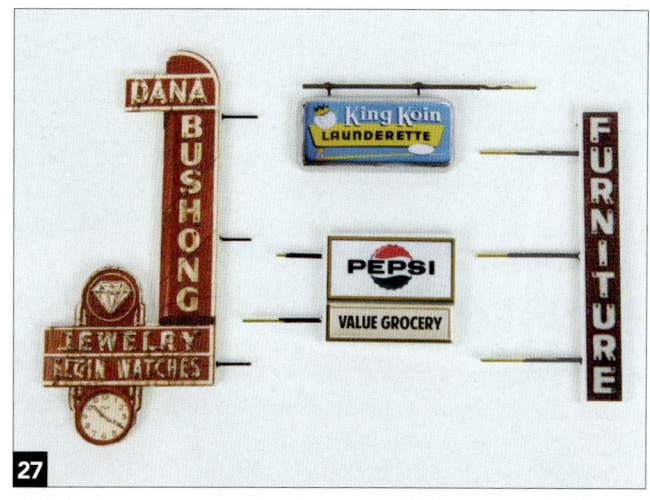

27 Vertical signs can use two or three poles or wires going directly from the edge of the sign to the building, while horizontal signs can use eye bolts and a horizontal arm.

28 Burnish the lettering to the white background with moderate pressure—just enough to get the lettering released from the backing paper to the wall.

29 Remove the backing paper slowly, making sure that the entire transfer has released from the paper to the wall.

Blair Line and others offer versions of these, signs but if you really want to make a building unique, it's fairly easy to make your own. I made my own projecting signs for several buildings in this book, starting with photos of real signs. If you get a photo from straight-on, very little work is needed—perhaps a bit of straightening in a graphics program (see chapter 8 for more details).

Determine the size needed and print out the graphic. This can vary by sides. Some signs are simply rectangles or shapes that match on each side, but some are shaped so that you'll need different graphics for each side. You can leave the graphics as is, or do as I did on the GE appliance store and Pepsi store signs and erase the original store name and swap in a new name.

Print out the signs at the desired size. I try to print out as many signs as possible at once to conserve paper (you can fit a lot of signs on a full-size sheet). Matte photo paper works well, and it resists fading and moisture better than regular paper, **22**.

I've found double-sided adhesive paper (made for mounting photos) also works well for these signs. Cut out around the sign, leaving ¼" or so around the edges. Cut a piece of mounting paper to match, peel off one side of the protective paper, and press the sign graphic in place. Trim the sign to its final size with small scissors or a hobby knife, **23**.

Cut the sign board itself from .080" styrene for HO signs (.040" for N and .100" or .125" for O). For complex shapes, trace the sign onto the plastic as a guide, **24**. File or sand the edges to smooth them, **25**.

Determine how you want to mount the sign. Most horizontal signs hang from a horizontal rod projecting from the building. For these, drill two no. 80 holes in the top of the sign board and glue wire eye bolts (Detail Associates no. 2206) in place, **26**. The .029" mounting rod (DA wire) will go through the eye bolts.

For vertical signs (or odd shapes, such as the GE sign), use two or three horizontal wires from the wall directly into the side of the sign, **27**. Either

30 Spray the background color in light coats over the sign and then remove the masking.

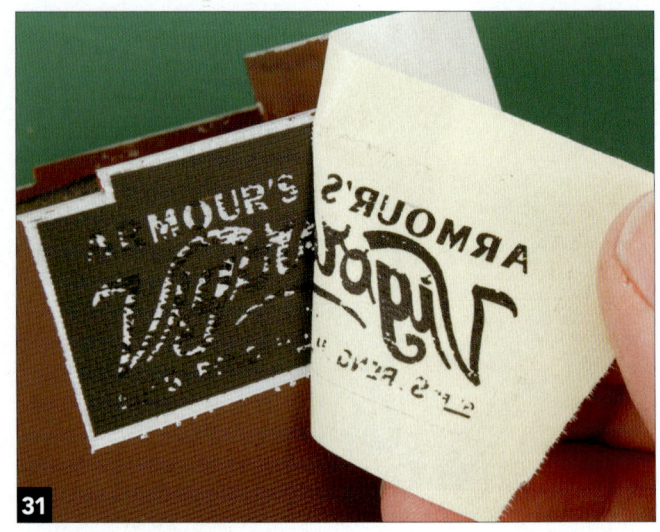

31 When the paint is dry to the touch, remove the transfer by pressing masking tape or gaffer tape over the dry transfer and peeling it off.

32 Repeat the process until all of the transfer material has been removed.

33 You can weather painted or decal signs with a wash of the wall or brick color, as here, or with chalk or an overspray.

way, to finish the sign, you can leave the styrene unpainted (many such signs had white housings) or paint the edges light gray or silver, then peel away the adhesive backing strip, and press the sign itself in place on each side.

Painted-on signs

Dry transfers can be used as a mask to create a true painted-on sign. This technique works for lettering-only signs with alphabet sets as well as for other graphics. I added an old advertising sign on the side wall of the brick storefront building shown in photo **1** with a Clover House dry transfer. The set (no. 8830-02) is actually designed for an early 1900s billboard refrigerator car, but the graphics seemed appropriate for an early 20th century sign that would be rather weathered for my 1960s-era building.

Start by brush-painting or airbrushing the background area the desired lettering color—white in this case. Burnish the dry transfers in place, **28**. Use enough pressure to transfer the graphics from the sheet to the surface but not so it bonds them securely to the wall, **29**.

Mask the area for the background color (black for this one). I masked over the edge of the white all the way around to provide a white border.

An airbrush or spray can is the best choice for adding the background color—apply the paint in very light coats. Keep the airbrush or spray can nozzle perpendicular to the surface to minimize the risk of paint bleeding under the transfers, **30**. You can use a brush, but you run a greater risk of paint bleed, and the transfers will be harder to remove.

As soon as the paint is dry to the touch, remove the transfers by pressing tape (masking or gaffer) to the surface and then peeling it up, **31**. It may take a few tries to get the last bits of transfer material off, **32**. You can carefully use a hobby knife to scrape off any particularly stubborn

34 Stir sticks often include lettering and designs with good potential for creating signs.

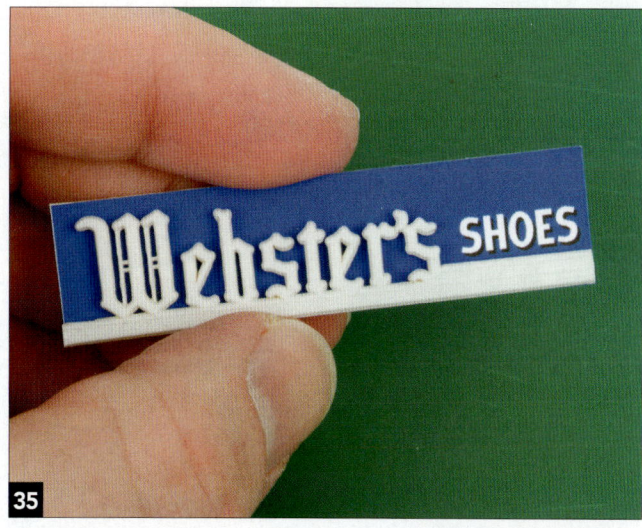

35 The Webster's Shoes sign is a combination of raised lettering and trim from a stir stick and a printed background and lettering.

pieces of transfer and touch up any areas, as needed, with a fine-point brush.

Because this sign was to appear old and faded, I added a weathering wash of the brick color thinned with water, **33**. You could get a similar effect with dark red chalk or a thinned weathering overspray. This weathering can be taken as far as you desire.

Stir stick signs
Stir sticks, or swizzle sticks, can be a great source of raised lettering as well as other items often found in fiberglass form in real life—note the crab, horse head, and rooster in photo **34**. Lettering can be found in a tremendous variety of styles and sizes. You can use the lettering as is, and simply cut it from the stick, or trim and rearrange the letters to make new words and business names.

I used the Eddie Webster's stir stick as the basis for a signboard for Webster's Shoes, **35**. I made the blue backing board, which includes the SHOES lettering, in Adobe Photoshop Elements, printed it out, and affixed it to .010" styrene. I glued the Webster's portion of the stick, along with part of the stick itself, to the backing board with cyanoacrylate adhesive (CA). I then glued the whole sign to the storefront, as seen in photo **1**.

Antique stores are great places to search for stir sticks. I've come across dozens of styles of them, and rarely paid more than a dollar or two apiece. You can also find them on eBay and other online sources.

Barber pole
I wanted to add a barber pole to the front of the barbershop seen in the photo on page 72. I started by printing out the classic pole striping on matte photo paper: blue/white/red/white in a repeating pattern. My HO pole is a scale 5 feet tall, with the striping about 3 feet tall.

I glued a section of the striping to a piece of 1/8" plastic tubing, and then thinned one end of the tube as much as I could with the end of a hobby knife. I glued the smallest steel ball bearing that I could find in the end of the tube with CA. I then wrapped the bottom with a bit of silver duct tape, but if I had it to do over, I'd probably use Bare Metal Foil or regular aluminum foil.

The mounting base on the building is a short length of C channel styrene glued to the building front with CA. I simply glued the pole to the channel, making sure the seam in the striping was at the rear.

81

CHAPTER EIGHT

Structures and flats from photos

Photos of prototype structures can be resized, printed out, and combined with model buildings. This HO Rexall drugstore has photo-print storefronts on two sides, which are mounted on a Design Preservation Models building.

Earlier projects in this book have shown how easy it is to use photos, scans, and imaging software to reproduce items such as signs, interior walls, and details. You can also use photos and graphics to produce entire building sides or complete structures, **1**.

2 This photo, a slide taken in the 1990s, was the starting point for my HO laundromat. The angle of the photo is good, but the problems are the car parked in front and the hanging sign, which obscures part of the building sign.

3 I edited the image in Photoshop Elements. I have already fixed the perspective with the Skew tool, and the Clone Stamp tool has taken care of most of the car and the top part of the hanging sign.

As well-detailed as many of today's structure kits are, and as good as we may be at painting and weathering these models, it still can be difficult to capture all the variations and minute details of some prototype structures, especially the appearance of brickwork and old weathered metal or wood siding.

Taking photos of these buildings, then resizing them, printing them, and assembling them can give you extremely realistic buildings that are unique to your layout. You can customize them with signs and other details on the computer, and combine them with other model details (window frames, door frames, loading docks, etc.) to help blend them with other structures.

You can also combine parts from different structures, such as taking a front wall from one building, side walls from another, and door or window frames or signs from still another.

The photo-realistic aspect makes these structures appear quite authentic, especially from a distance, where the lack of three-dimensional detail isn't readily apparent.

Starting photos

You need a good photo or two of the prototype structure that you're modeling. The best option, if a building still exists, is to take digital photos yourself. If you're taking photos with modeling in mind, a lightly overcast day is often the best—sunny days result in brighter colors, but also leave dark shadows that can be difficult to fix or hide.

Use a standard-length or smaller telephoto lens (somewhere from 50mm to 85mm) if possible to limit distortion of straight lines in the photo. Take the photo from straight on, centering yourself with the wall, again to limit distortion. Do this with each of the building's walls.

If there are objects in the way, such as parked cars or trucks, light poles, or mailboxes, take photos from several vantage points. This will allow you to choose the best viewpoint later, and also give you the option of blending two or more photos to eliminate the objects.

Over the past several years, I've tried to get into the habit of photographing any old or interesting structures that catch my eye, with the thought that someday they might make good modeling subjects. These photos don't have to be of a complete structure. For example, a photo of a large brick wall is an excellent starting point toward creating another building.

Another option is to scan older color photographs and slides. This is likely your only option if the building no longer exists or has been extensively remodeled. The more straight-on that these are taken, the better, and you'll be able to correct quite a bit of perspective distortion with photo-editing software. Scan these images at high resolution to preserve as much detail as possible.

You can sometimes find usable photos of structures via the Internet. The Library of Congress photo collection is a great place to search (loc.gov/pictures), and you can find many high-resolution color images of structures and signs dating back to the 1940s. Be aware that many photos on the web are low-resolution (typically 72 ppi, or pixels per inch). To print well, a photo should be at least 150 ppi (preferably 240 ppi) at the size you'll be using it.

Be aware of copyright laws when using photos from the web. Remember that the copyright rests with the person who took the photo. You can typically use any photo you find for your personal use, but you do not have the right to distribute the photo (or anything you've made from that photo) to others, regardless of whether you charge for them.

Straighten and size

Once you have your photos, come up with a plan for the structure. As an example, here's what I did to turn a photo into a structure for an HO scale scene. My original image was a slide that I shot in the 1990s of the King Koin Launderette in LaMars, Iowa, **2**. King Koin was a Midwestern chain

83

4 The Clone Stamp tool removed all signs of the car and helped fill in the missing letters on the building sign. The image is now ready to print.

5 For the laundromat's side wall, I decided to use part of a brick wall from an industrial building. The advertising signs add interest.

6 The finished prints are ready to be turned into a model. Matte photo paper is the best choice for doing this, to ensure a flat finish.

7 The building shell is simply a box made from .100" styrene sheet with a recessed roof. The roof is painted black and the wall caps gray, with detail items glued in place.

of laundromats, and the building in LaMars had a distinctive tile front and cool-looking tin sign spanning the tops of the windows and doors.

I scanned the slide at 3600 ppi on my desktop scanner, which provided plenty of resolution for an HO building. If you don't have a scanner, you can have a graphics design service do this for you.

I opened the scan of the front wall in Adobe Photoshop Elements (which I find extremely versatile and, at around or under $100, a pretty good bargain). Other photo-editing software will perform similar tasks, but the names of various actions and menu items will differ.

Commercial products

If you don't have photos of your own to get going with these techniques—or if you want more options—several companies offer software, digital files, and ready-printed cardstock and paper products for making structures.

CG Textures (cgtextures.com) offers a wide variety of wall and roof textures, along with doors, windows, signs, carpeting, rugs, drapes, and entire walls, as well as landscapes and roads.

Evan Designs offers software (modeltrainsoftware.com) for making your own paper structures, including many textures and components, and the company also offers paper kits.

KingMill Enterprises (kingmill.3dcartstores.com) offers the Radical Flats line of photo-realistic cardstock components, including building walls, flats, roofs, and entire structure kits.

Other companies offering digital files of textures or card buildings include 3DK (3dk.ca), Clever Models (clever-models.net), modelbuildings.org, scalemodelplans.com, and scalescenes.com.

8 Double-check the size of each wall printout to the actual building shell.

9 Adhere the print to one side of the peel-and-stick paper, then remove the backing sheet from the other side.

10 Carefully align the print to the wall at the bottom, then tip it upward into place.

11 Press the graphic firmly in place. Trim the top and any edges as needed, and repeat the process with each wall.

The best way to learn photo editing is to simply play with the program. Many photo-driven and video tutorials are online (check YouTube), most of which are geared to specific functions. Also check with your friends—chances are that someone you know uses Photoshop and can be bribed to help you get started.

Save the image with a different name (never edit an original image, in case you need to go back to the beginning). Start by straightening the image. My photo was taken close to straight-on, but the outward lines (the vertical edges of the walls and the wall's top and bottom) weren't parallel with each other. The Transform>Skew function lets you grab each corner and move it in, out, up, or down to correct this. Turning on the Grid function allows you to see how the edges are aligning, ensuring that they become square with each other.

Next, clean up the image as much as possible. In my photo, a car was parked in front of the building, which obscured a large part of it. I used the Clone Stamp tool to copy the tile pattern (and then window) from visible areas over the car, and I repeated the process until the car was gone, **3**.

Also with the Clone Stamp tool, I cleaned up some cracked tile pieces, added an extra column of tile at each side that I could wrap around to the sides of the building, removed the edge of the hanging sign, and cleaned up the flat tin sign. I darkened some of the faded letters with the pencil tool. I set the color to black and the opacity to about 40 percent so I could use multiple passes to gradually revive the lettering but still leave it somewhat faded.

Go to Image>Resize>Image Size and save the image at the size you need for the finished structure. If you know the dimensions of the building, this is easy. If you're not sure, as was the case for this one, try to determine the size of something in the photo. I used the height of the entry door: 80" (6'-8") is common for these, so I went with that and sized the rest of the front to match. When you're done, save the image as a JPG or TIFF file, **4**.

12 The finished structure makes up for its lack of 3D details with its photo-realistic appearance.

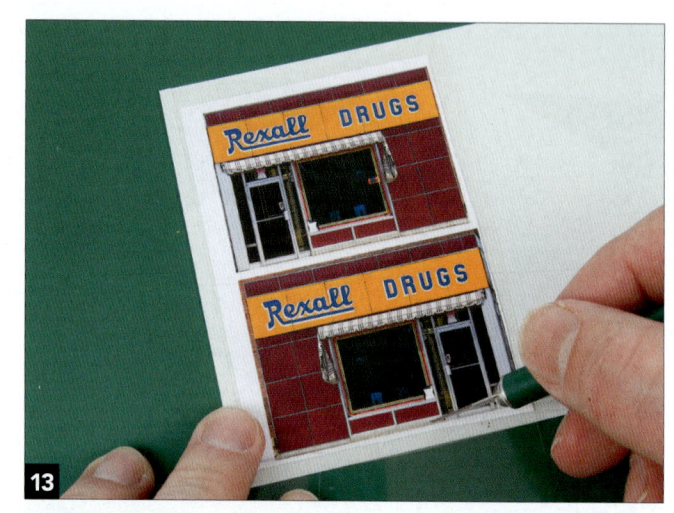

13 Use double-sided mounting paper to mount the storefront graphics on thin (.010") styrene sheet. Trim them to size with a straightedge and hobby knife.

14 Use a knife and file to remove any protruding details that interfere with the new graphic at the front of the structure.

15 Lightly mark the location of the graphic on the side of the building. Smooth the area with a large flat file.

Since I only had a photo of the front of the laundromat, I had to come up with something for one side (the rear and other side will be hidden, as this building abuts an adjoining structure). Many buildings like this have tile and other "fancy" treatments (enameled panels, polished brick, etc.) only at the front, with the sides being rather plain.

I looked through files of structure photos I'd already taken and found a shot of the side of a large (two-story) industrial building, **5**. The wall was brick, with old advertising signs (Mail Pouch tobacco and 7-Up) painted on it. I decided to use a small portion of it for the visible wall.

I repeated the editing process for the side wall. After straightening the image with the Skew function, I resized it, based on a standard brick's height (with mortar) at about 3 courses = 8". I wanted to include the large 7-Up sign, figuring that it would have been a realistic billboard-style wall sign for a building side facing a parking lot. I made sure the sign's height matched the height of the front wall.

Print your images on matte photo paper, **6**. I use a high-end inkjet printer, but even newer consumer-model printers do a good job with images. Obviously the better quality the printer, the better your images and the resulting model will be. Again, a graphics house or photo lab can do this for you as well.

Putting it together

This basic structure required only a simple box, **7**. I assembled a box from .100" styrene sheet, using techniques described in chapter 4. I recessed the roof (another styrene piece) between the side walls and angled it downward slightly from front to back. The roof is simply painted grimy black, with black lines painted across it to represent seams in the roofing material. The tops of the front and side walls are painted concrete. The chimney is from a City Classics detail set (no. 208), and the two vents are from Walthers' excellent roof detailing set (no. 933-3733).

Make sure the dimensions match the printouts, **8**. Because the photo included the window and door details,

16 The structure is ready for the new storefronts. The one on the front will simply cover the original windows and door.

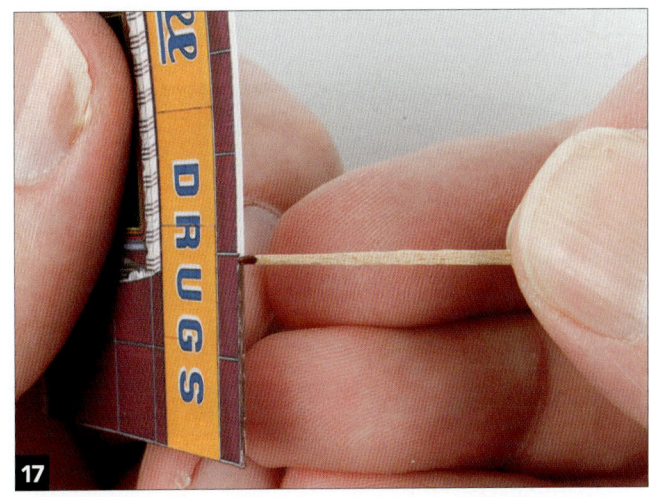

17 Touch up the edges of the new storefronts with matching paint: maroon on the top and outside, orange along the sign, and aluminum along the mating edges.

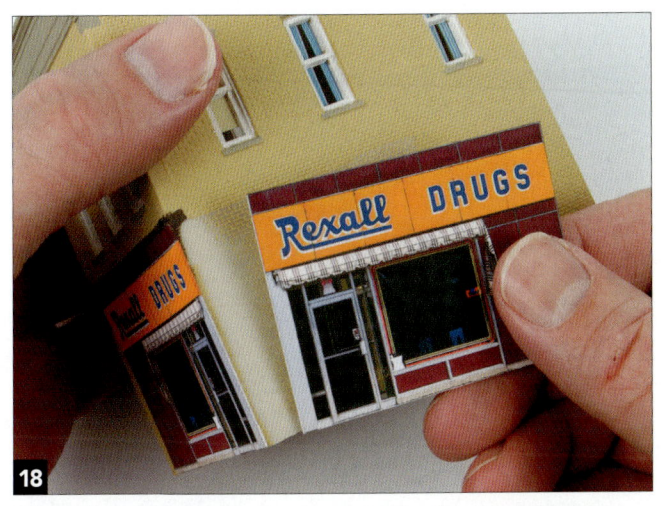

18 Add gel-type liquid plastic cement to the front mounting surfaces and add the new storefront, making sure it's aligned properly. Follow by adding the new piece to the side.

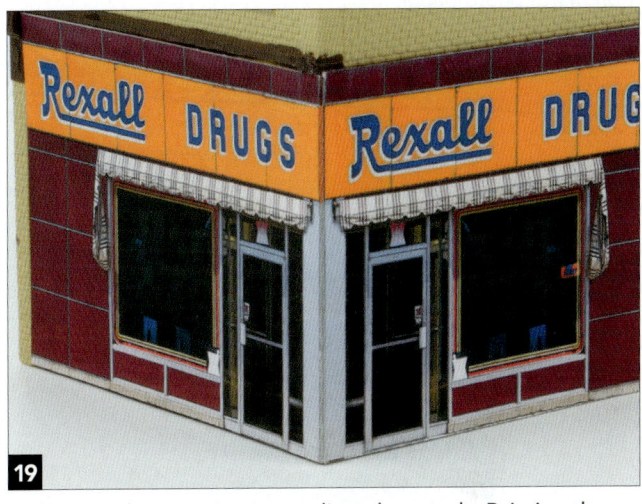

19 Make sure the two pieces are aligned correctly. Painting the edges helps ensure a good-looking corner joint.

the shell didn't require any window openings or special treatment.

You can glue the prints in place, but my favorite method of mounting a print to plastic is using double-sided mounting paper. It's available in sheets with two peel-and-stick sides. (I use Stick'M from Model Builders Supply, modelbuilderssupply.com.) Its main advantage is that it holds securely and instantly, with no bubbling under the print surface and no risk of liquid glue wrinkling the paper. Its disadvantage is that you get just one chance to place it—once the adhesive grabs, your only recourse for missed placement is to scrape it off and start over with a new print.

Cut a piece of mounting paper slightly larger than the print for the front of the structure. Peel one side of the protective covering from the adhesive sheet, and on a smooth, flat surface, press the print firmly to the sheet. Use a straightedge and hobby knife to trim the print to its final size.

Test-fit the print to the wall. I had the structure shell on a flat surface, so I could position the print at the bottom and then lean it up into place. Remove the adhesive backing, **9**, carefully position the print, **10**, and press it in place, **11**. Repeat the process for the other walls.

I made the hanging sign from another photo, as described in chapter 7. I drilled a mounting hole in the front of the building and glued the sign mounting wire in place.

This building is one of several in a city block, so I didn't go to any special lengths to detail it, **12**. If it were a foreground structure, I would have considered cutting out the window openings, adding clear glazing behind them, and possibly adding a bit of interior detail behind the windows. The level of detailing you want to do is up to you.

Combining prints and structure kits

You can also apply a photo or graphics to a kit or ready-built structure. I did this with a corner Rexall store and an HO Design Preservation Models kit (no. 10100, Kelly's Saloon). This

20 The D.P. Wigley building is another structure that started as a digital photograph. After correcting the perspective and cleaning the image (removing a few signs and wires), I printed it on matte photo paper.

21 Spray adhesive, such as 3M Super 77, works well for securing larger prints to backdrops and mounting boards. Give the back of the print an even coat.

22 I mounted the print on a piece of black mat board, and then used a utility knife to cut out the outline of the building. The piece of thick black foam core is optional—it allows you to mount the flat away from the backdrop.

23 Here's the finished flat, ready for installation. The photos in the background are attached directly to the backdrop.

actually parallels prototype practice, where the old cast-iron fronts on many older brick buildings were modernized with porcelain panels.

I treated the drugstore photo as I did the one of the laundromat, correcting the perspective and cleaning a few items (lamppost and sign) from the photo. Had I thought it through, I would have joined the walls side-to-side so they could have been folded to create a seamless corner. As it was, I printed them as two separate pieces on matte photo paper, **13**. This just made it more of a challenge to hide the corner joint.

Mount both storefront graphics to .010" styrene using double-sided mounting paper. This makes it easier to attach them to the structure.

I had assembled and painted the structure years ago for a long-forgotten project. I prepped it by shaving off some protruding details from the front, gluing styrene strips around the door and windows to provide a level surface, and filing the side of the building where the side graphic goes, **14** and **15**. As photo **16** shows, this doesn't have to be perfectly smooth—just enough to provide a good gluing surface for the graphic.

Paint the edges of the new storefronts to match the graphics, **17**—you don't want white styrene or the edges of the photo paper distracting from the storefront graphics.

Test-fit the new storefronts and then glue them in place with liquid plastic cement, **18**. Make sure they align properly at the corner, **19**. The finished building is shown in photo **1**.

Building flats

This technique also works well for building flats. Building a flat is just what it sounds like: a single wall, mounted directly to the backdrop or

24 I had 18" x 24" poster prints made, each including several large structure images. Poster prints are an economical way to make large building flats.

on a spacing board just off a backdrop. Flats can be layered, mounted at angles, and shown at angles to provide perspective as well. Flats can be combined with full and partial structures, and they can have additional details added to them.

The D.P. Wigley building in photo **20** is one example. Another HO project, it's much larger than the laundromat—about 9" wide and 7" tall. I started with a straight-on digital photo that I had taken. I cleaned up the door openings and windows, making them uniform in appearance. I also used the Clone Stamp tool to remove a couple of wires that were hanging in front of the building. I then printed the flat on matte photo paper.

I mounted the print on black mat board by spraying the back with 3M Super 77 adhesive and pressing it in place on the mat board, **21**. I then cut out the building using a utility knife and a steel straightedge. Since this flat will be mounted slightly off the backdrop, I glued a piece of thick black foam core to the back, **22**. This acts as a spacer and also lets the flat stand up, **23**. Chapter 9 shows how this flat is combined with a low-relief structure and other prints to create a scene.

You can do even larger structures with this technique, **24**. Don't feel limited by your own photo printer, as you can have prints done commercially. The disadvantage of this is having to wait to see the results. Another economical method for making large flats or structures is having them printed as poster prints. I use shortrunposters.com, which offers very reasonable prices for 18" x 24" and 24" x 36" prints (there are other companies out there as well). The images aren't quite as sharp as photographic prints, but for background structures, this usually isn't critical.

Check local graphics supply houses, and you'll find companies that can make prints (for long buildings or entire backdrops) in a continuous length. This allows you to blend the sky and fill an entire wall along a layout.

Chapter 9 contains examples of how to blend backdrops, flats, and low-relief structures to create scenes.

CHAPTER NINE

Finishing scenes

A key to having a realistic building is that it looks like it belongs in a scene. It must be blended with the scenery and surrounding details. This Walthers HO grain elevator rests on a foundation that was planted prior to adding the building.

After you've built some nice structures, you need to get them realistically blended into your layout. There are several ways to do this, and it is important to make sure they have a solid foundation to rest upon and that they don't look like they were merely placed on top of the scenery, **1**.

2 For this HO city block, I used two rows of Walthers street system sidewalk sections. This gives the structures a level base at the fronts and sides.

3 Make sure the structure's rear and sides are supported at the same level as the front. Styrene strip works well for this.

4 A drop of CA at each corner is enough to secure a structure. Make sure the structure sits flat and is aligned properly.

5 Make sure buildings with their own bases have the base at the same height as the sidewalk. Trim or shim the base if needed.

City structures

For structures along a city street, the challenge is to generally keep everything level and even so that the buildings sit on their bases with no gaps. Start with a level sub-base. For example, photo 2 shows an HO city scene being built on a plywood base. (You can see the finished scene in photos on pages 55 and 59.) The street and sidewalks here are Walthers concrete street system components, but the same techniques apply regardless of the street and sidewalk materials.

For buildings in cities and towns, it's usually a good idea to discard sidewalks attached to structures or structure bases: no two are the same, and it's impossible to get neighboring buildings to match. You want to have a level sidewalk that also serves as a structure base.

I used a double layer of the Walthers sidewalk pieces, which gives the front of the structure (and the side of a building on a corner) a solid base, **2**. It also provides a sidewalk under exposed areas for buildings that have recessed entryways. For the rear of the building, add a piece of strip or sheet styrene that matches the height of the sidewalk pieces, **3**. Test-fit the building, making sure there are no gaps on any side, **4**. File or shave off any imperfections in the sidewalk or structure bottom that keep it from sitting properly. Repeat the process along the block.

For buildings that have their own bases, make sure that the base matches the depth of the sidewalk. I had to use a knife and file to trim a bit of material from the base of the Walthers store shown in photo **5**. Also, the second layer of sidewalk was not needed, as the building had its own sidewalk for the recessed area toward the entry door, **6**.

I like to secure my city buildings with just a single drop of cyanoacrylate adhesive (CA) applied out-of-sight at each corner. This keeps them in place if they get bumped, but they're also easy to remove if needed to replace an interior light, add details, or change signs.

You can also mount a building—or a group of buildings—on a base prior to installation. This base can include scenery as well. I added a Woodland Scenics HO Corner Emporium building to a foam core base, and included an adjoining empty lot, **7**. This made it easier to add to some uneven terrain by simply adding shims under the base until it was level, **8**.

By painting the edge of the base a concrete color, the visible part looks like a foundation and step, **9**. The layout scenery can later be blended to the base.

Stand-alone buildings

For buildings served by rail spurs, make sure the structure is at the proper height to match a railcar on

6 When in place, buildings should blend in with the sidewalk and have no gaps.

7 You can mount structures, like this HO Woodland Scenics built-up, on a base prior to installing them.

8 A couple of foam core shims on hilly scenery, in this case carved foam, allows the structure base to sit level.

9 Painted a concrete color, the exposed base at the front of the store looks like a step.

10 Once the building is in place, bring the scenery to it. Placing matte medium along the seam holds coarse ground foam on the right side. The bare cork and building base seam along the loading dock at left will be covered by additional matching ballast.

11 Once the scenery materials are added, the building looks like it is part of the scenery.

92

12 The styrene base for the elevator includes a wood floor for the truck driveway. The edge of the styrene is painted a concrete color.

13 Glue the foundation to the layout base, making sure it's level, and then add scenery around it. The other platform represents a truck scale.

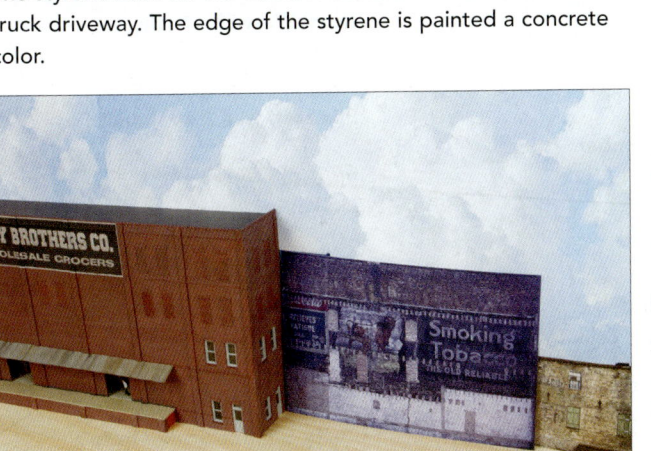

14 I positioned two different structure prints against the backdrop, trying to see what would look best combined with the 3-D structure.

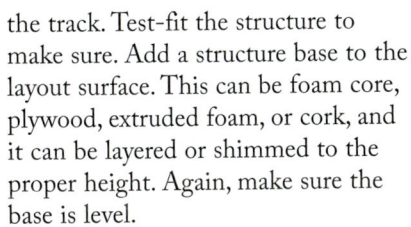

15 The D.P. Wigley flat is another poster print, mounted on matboard and spaced away from the backdrop with ¾" foam core.

the track. Test-fit the structure to make sure. Add a structure base to the layout surface. This can be foam core, plywood, extruded foam, or cork, and it can be layered or shimmed to the proper height. Again, make sure the base is level.

Bring the scenery to the edge of the structure base and then add the structure. Add several drops of CA or white glue to hold it securely. Blend the scenery to the base of the structure with ground foam, ballast, or crushed rock, **10**. The glue holding the scenery materials also helps keep the building in place, **11**.

Separate bases
You can customize a structure base and foundation and secure it to the layout, blend scenery to it, and then add the structure. I did this with the HO Walthers grain elevator in photo **1**. I made a foundation from .100" styrene sheet, cut to match the building's footprint, and then added a wood deck to the truck lean-to floor with Midwest scribed wood, **12**. I stained and weathered it as described in chapter 6.

I glued the base to the layout, made sure it was level, and then added scenery up to it, **13**. The building can then be set or glued in place. This allows you to do scenery work without having the structure or structures in the way.

Low-relief buildings and flats
The May Brothers building from chapter 3 was designed as a low-relief building that fits against a backdrop. This is a handy way to get large buildings in tight spaces, as in a city or industrial scene. To make the building blend into the backdrop and give the impression that the scene is larger, I blended it with a couple of structure flats: photos or walls placed directly on the backdrop.

I played with a couple of arrangements, using poster prints of structures made as described in chapter 8, **14**. I glued the prints to the backdrop using Super 77 spray, applying it to the back of each print, and then carefully pressing it in place. After adding the May building, I added another flat to the other end of the building, this time spacing it slightly off the backdrop, **15**.

The possibilities for combining full-size buildings, low-relief structures, prints, and flats are endless. Use your imagination and test-fit arrangements to see what you can come up with.

List of manufacturers

Alexander Scale Models (see Tomar)

American Model Builders
laserkit.com

Bachmann Industries
bachmanntrains.com

Badger Air-Brush Co.
badgerairbrush.com

Bar Mills Models
barmillsmodels.com

Blair Line
blairline.com

B.T.S. Structures
btsrr.com

Campbell Scale Models
campbellscalemodels.com

City Classics
cityclassics.biz

Clover House
cloverhouse.com

Design Preservation Models
(see Woodland Scenics)

Detail Associates (see Walthers)

Downtown Deco
downtowndeco.com

Evan Designs
evandesignsmodelbuilder.com

Evergreen Scale Models
evergreenscalemodels.com

Faller (see Walthers)

GC Laser
gclaser.com

Gold Medal Models
goldmm.com

Grandt Line
grandtline.com

Great West Models
greatwestmodels.com

JL Innovative Design
jlinnovativedesign.com

K&S Engineering
ksmetals.com

Kappler Scale Lumber
kapplerusa.com

Kibri (see Walthers)

Kitwood Hill Models
kitwoodhillmodels.com

Krylon
krylon.com

Lunde Studios
lundestudios.com

Micro Engineering
microengineering.com

Micro-Mark
micromark.com

Microscale Decals
microscale.com

Midwest Products
midwestproducts.com

Miller Engineering
microstru.com

Miniatronics
miniatronics.com

Model Power
modelpower.com

Model Tech Studios
modeltechstudios.com

Monster Modelworks
monstermodelworks.com

Noch (see Walthers)

Northeastern Scale Lumber
northeasternscalelumber.com

NorthWest Short Line
nwsl.com

Pikestuff (see Rix Products)

Plastruct
plastruct.com

Preiser (see Walthers)

Rix Products
rixproducts.com

Rusty Stumps Scale Models
rustystumps.com

Scalecoat Paint
weavermodels.com

Scale Structures Ltd.
scale-structures.com

Smalltown USA (see Rix Products)

Special Shapes
specialshapes.com

Testor Corp.
testors.com

Tomar Industries
tomarindustries.com

Wm. K. Walthers
walthers.com

Woodland Scenics
woodlandscenics.com

X-Acto
xacto.com

About the author

Jeff Wilson has written more than 30 books on railroads and model railroading. He spent 10 years as an associate editor at *Model Railroader* magazine, and he currently works as a freelance writer, editor, and photographer, contributing articles to MR and other magazines.

He enjoys many facets of the hobby, especially building structures and detailing locomotives, as well as photographing both real and model railroads.

Acknowledgements

Thanks go out to several companies and individuals who helped me with projects by providing materials and other assistance: Atlas Model Railroad Co. (Paul Graf), Bachmann Industries, Bar Mills Models (Art Fahie), Blair Line (Dale Rush), City Classics (Jim Sacco), Classic Metal Works/Mini Metals, Coffman Engineering, GC Laser Innovations, Cody Grivno, JL Innovative Design (Dave Proell), Kent Johnson, Micro-Mark (Tom Picarillo), Microscale, NorthWest Short Line, Rix/Smalltown (Rick Rideout), Wm. K. Walthers (Kara Yanacheck), and Woodland Scenics.

Know the Essentials

Inside Kalmbach's "Essentials Series" books you'll find everything you need to know to get started in model railroading and improve your layouts.

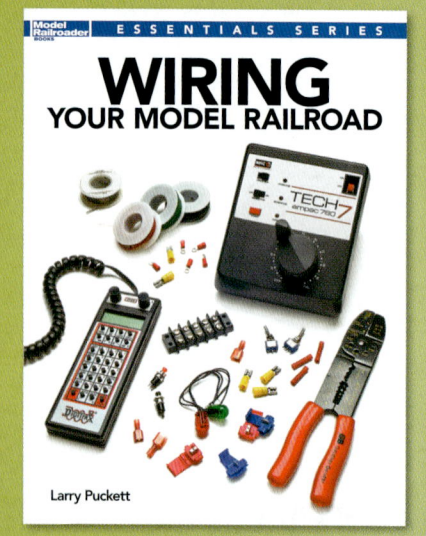

WIRING YOUR MODEL RAILROAD
#12491 • $21.99

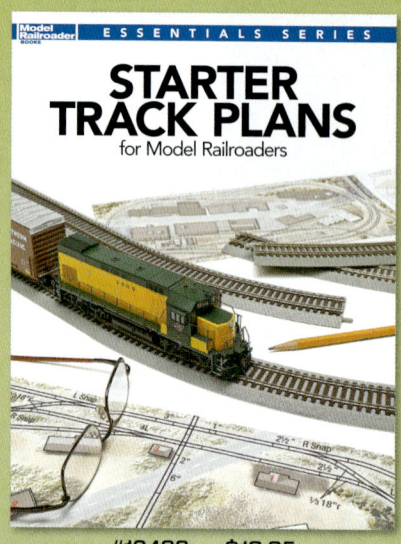

STARTER TRACK PLANS for Model Railroaders
#12466 • $16.95

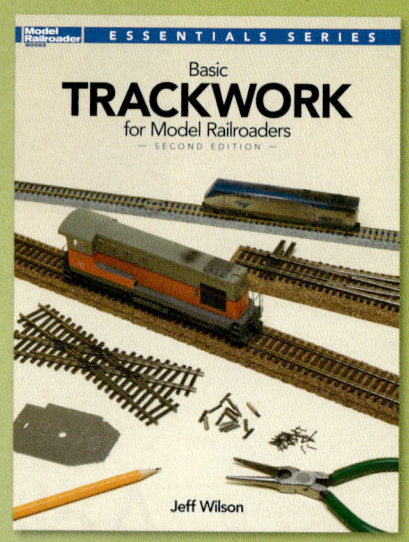

Basic TRACKWORK for Model Railroaders — SECOND EDITION —
#12479 • $19.99

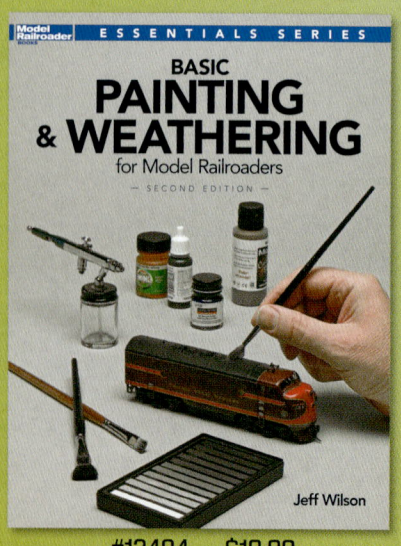

BASIC PAINTING & WEATHERING for Model Railroaders — SECOND EDITION —
#12484 • $19.99

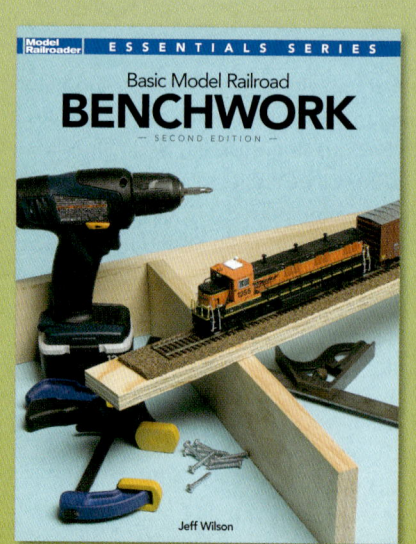

Basic Model Railroad BENCHWORK — SECOND EDITION —
#12469 • $19.95

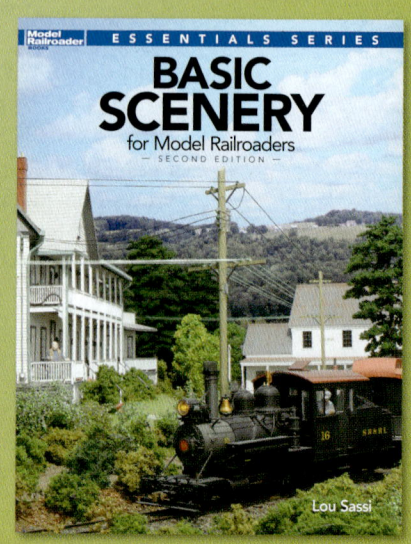

BASIC SCENERY for Model Railroaders — SECOND EDITION —
#12482 • $19.99

Buy now from your local hobby shop!
Shop at KalmbachHobbyStore.com

KB Kalmbach Books

2XMRR